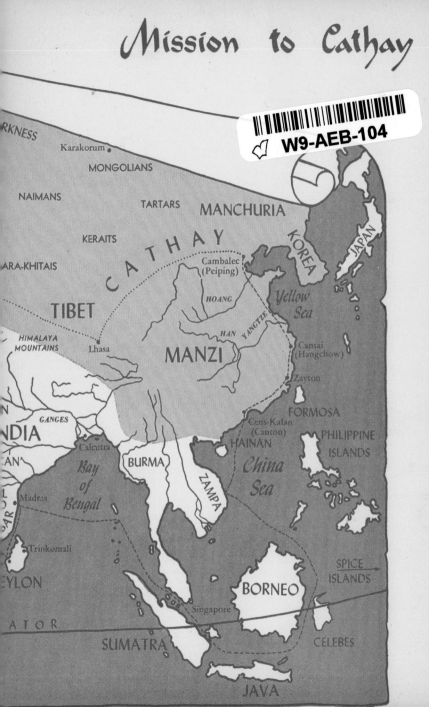

Mission to Cathay

Mission to 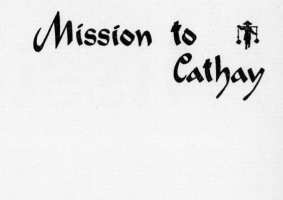 Cathay

THE BIOGRAPHY OF

Mission

Anselm M. Romb, O.F.M. Conv.

BLESSED ODORIC OF PORDENONE

to Cathay

1956

St. Anthony Guild Press, Paterson, New Jersey

B
O

ACKNOWLEDGMENTS

My sincerest gratitude to those confreres of the Friars Minor Conventual who have helped me so signally with this work: to Martin Ignatowski, for typing the manuscript; to Norbert Rackensperger, for proofreading it; and to Firmin Finn, Hubert Kamler, and Leo Gabriel Neal, for various kinds of aid in preparing it for publication; finally, to William D'Arcy, for making my research so easy and pleasant.

Anselm M. Romb, O. F. M. Conv.

FEAST OF ST. BONAVENTURE
JULY 14, 1955

CONTENTS

Mission to Cathay

CHAPTER 1

By Way of Introduction

 The history of ideas, not of dates, is the real chronicle of mankind. Events are only concrete expressions of the passage of history from mind to mind.

One idea that helped write the chronicle of Europe for a long time is ordinarily neglected by historians. This is the tradition of the early Middle Ages that the year 1000 would witness the second coming of Christ. Whether we like it or not, we cannot ignore the influence of religion in the Dark Ages. Most of all, we cannot blame those ages for *wanting* the second coming, the millennium, the reign of the peace of Christ.

As Rome backed away from barbarian conquerors many generations earlier, good management in business and law disintegrated. In a short time Europe was staggering from economic hunger and anarchy. Only its belief in things unseen, its hope of heavenly repayment for suffering on earth, held it to some kind of rational order.

Pope St. Gregory the Great (590-604), the mentor of
the West midway between Augustine and Bernard, gives
us no small indication of the keenly expected coming of
Christ, in his *First Homily on the Gospel* (Luke 21:
25-33):

> Our Lord and Redeemer wished to find us ready [for His
> second coming]. He tells us what evils will come upon the aging
> world in order to curb our love for it. He points out what afflic-
> tions will announce *the nearing end of the world*. Thus if we
> refuse to fear God in times of peace, at least in times of affliction
> we will fear *His close judgment*. . . . Our Lord said that nation will
> rise against nation, and kingdom against kingdom: and there will
> be great earthquakes everywhere, and pestilence and famine. . . .
> He added that there will be signs in the sun and moon and stars;
> on the earth the press of nations because of the confusion from
> the sound of the sea and the waves. Indeed, we are already
> witnessing some of these signs; others *we await with trembling in
> the near future*. We see nation rising against nation and their rest-
> lessness all over the earth even in our own times [the barbarian
> invasions] — more, in fact, than we read about in the codices
> [of the Gospel]. You know how often we have heard of earth-
> quakes destroying countless cities in other regions of the earth. We
> are suffering pestilence without end. We see no obvious signs
> in the sun and moon and stars so far, it is true. But we know
> these too are *close at hand* from the present changes in the atmos-
> phere.[1]

This is the sentiment of the Dark Ages. Not even
the order restored by Charlemagne at the end of the
eighth century served to dispel the hope of the millennium.
Charlemagne's influence on the foreboding attitude of
Europe was of short duration. With the second coming

---

1. Translation by the writer from the *Breviarium Romano-Seraphicum,*
First Sunday of Advent, Third Nocturn: Lessons VII-IX.

of Christ so near, they thought, there was not much point in building for the future.

Once the 1000 mark was left behind, the morbid senti- ment of earlier days seemed to dissolve in relief. If the world wasn't going to end after all, why not make a fresh beginning? Europe took to growing up all over again.

First-century Europe had the one government of Rome and many religions. Eleventh-century Europe had many governments and the one religion of Rome. The over-all framework was different: the note of universality was with the Church, not with the State.

Because they shared a common way of doing things, people of the same region drew together and shared their political destiny too. That is the story of the consolidation of nations. Ambitious leaders could never have made those they conquered into one people if the people had not been united somehow already. Once more the his- torical event followed the historical idea as its external sign.

When the nearness of the *next* world had ceased to trouble men, they became progressively more interested in how much security *this* world could be made to yield. Bankers established houses of trade and credit and insurance even in the twelfth century. Towns called themselves communes and built reputations for the crafts they practiced. Like state and county fairs of rural areas today, the medieval fairs brought local products together to be sold in large or small quantities.

Guilds of merchants had even a kind of stock exchange by the thirteenth century. Kings and cities issued their

own coinage. The Knights Templars, originally founded
to wage holy wars, made moneylending their avocation.
The old houses of nobility scorned cheap traffic in the
world's goods and looked down their noses at burghal
society. But they knew where to go for money.

More than anything else, the Crusades broadened
European horizons. The year 1000 did not see Christ
come Himself to claim the Holy Places from Islam. Therefore, Christians reasoned, they ought to claim the Holy
Places in the name of Christ. Urban II preached the First
Crusade from Clermont in 1095. The foreign campaigns
certainly relieved Europe of thousands of petty, warring
nobles. If they survived, the nobles brought back enough
booty to pay the moneylenders and to get a start in business themselves.

The Kingdom of Jerusalem was founded by the Crusaders in 1099. It was a listening post that cocked the ears
of Europe eastward. The Near East, men learned with
astonishment, was merely a hallway to the mansions of
the East. In fact, Europe could be swallowed up in a
corner of some Far Eastern Empire with scarcely a notice
at all.

More than commerce and knowledge of geography in-
creased after 1000. Universities made their earliest appearance at this time. Philosophy, theology, canon law,
political science, natural science: these were taught at the
"graduate schools" of Europe. The beauty and truth of
the Greek and Roman classics once more took their
rightful place in the accumulative tradition of Western
civilization.

The later Middle Ages, so much in contrast with the Dark Ages, expressed this new vitality in exuberant art forms. The smallest towns had to have monumental churches; the cathedrals of the cities still continue to amaze us. Lifelike sculpture and perspective in painting, though still mostly religious, indicate how art itself was interpreted from a more earthly point of view. Austere Gregorian chant lost ground before the "new art" of measured rhythm and harmony.

All of this is good. Our citizenship in heaven does not make us alien to earth. It is a warped mind that thinks education and progress devitalize holiness. Every truth discovered in the natural order is a reflection of the supernatural. Every effort of men as creatures of reason prepares them better to fulfill their destiny as creatures of grace.

This is the background of ideas against which we have to set Blessed Odoric of Pordenone. He was born into a Europe that achieved an envious balance between flesh and spirit. One can call it *post-millennium* Europe. We can understand Odoric's activities better if we remember the general enthusiasm of which he is a part.

Many early Franciscans, as we shall have occasion to repeat, were lured to exotic lands. Adventure, chivalry, knighthood: none of these is out of place in holy lives. On the contrary, they are necessary in Franciscan lives.

CHAPTER 2

From Sea to Sea

 A mission to Cathay in the thirteenth and fourteenth centuries spelled a mission to its Mongol overlords. And the popes and kings of medieval Europe sent more ambassadors to Cathay than we may suspect. Odoric had several predecessors among his confriars who dared the ill-treatment and the dangers of travel in the Far East.

The Mongols and Tartars were originally two separate tribes that lived in the cold tundras north of Cathay. But historians have applied both names indiscriminately to either group, and finally to the nomads they united. Often these tribal names were applied to the Oriental peoples of Cathay, who were the last large group to fall under Mongolian or Tartar domination.

Cathay, the destination of Odoric's missionary journeys and the center of Mongolian-Chinese culture, was that region of China which lay west of the

Yellow Sea for a couple of hundred miles inland. The Cathayans subsequently swallowed up their conquerors from the north because of Cathay's superior numbers and higher civilization. The Mongols who took Cathay with fire and sword were themselves defeated by too much civilization and luxury.

Genghis Khan (1162-1227), the prime mover of this consolidation of the Asiatic nomads, founded his dynasty about the same time St. Francis of Assisi founded his Order. They spent their lives simultaneously. They both set out with a single eye on world conquest. The outcome of these two parallel lives is that Genghis Khan's career was undone and largely forgotten, whereas Francis' career was multiplied and will never be forgotten where there are Christians. Yet the impress of neither man can be effaced from the history and exchange of ideas.

Tartar or Mongolian history begins with Genghis Khan. First he conquered his neighbors at home by persuasion or violence. As a unit the tribesmen pushed into Cathay and Manchuria, as well as to the west as far as the Danube River. When Kublai Khan — the emperor who figures so largely in Marco Polo's recollections — ascended the throne in 1259, he extended his power throughout China and ruled the mightiest empire in the chronicles of mankind.

Kublai Khan was dead when Odoric began his travels. The ruling Great Khan held immediate sway in Cathay and Manzi,[1] and over all the Mongols or Tartars from

---

1. Manzi, China's other principal division at that time, was south of Cathay. See map.

Manchuria southward and from Tibet eastward. Nominally under the Great Khan, other khans of lesser dignity ruled across the steppes to the Black Sea and down to the Persian Gulf. In this real sense, the Great Empire extended "from sea to sea."

Odoric knew the ferocity of the people to whom God was to call him. Their cruelty had been a byword in Europe for a man's lifetime. Europeans thought the very name "Tartar" was derived from *Tartarus,* which is a Latin word for hell. When one of the Tartar armies took a town, they plundered the place, burned it, and slaughtered every living person who could not serve as slave or craftsman. Neither age nor sex protected the unfortunates. Torture and debauchery, rioting and profaning of sacred places, were the order of the day. It was proverbial that only the smell of decaying bodies could drive off the victors.

Worst of all to bear was the bravado of the barbarians: their god ordained their victories and gave them the whole world in vassalage. Those who refused to crawl to Tartar feet disobeyed heaven itself. As Tacitus had written of the Teutons, the Tartars too left desolation behind them and called it peace.

Despite what he knew of them, Odoric's purpose in life was single: if the Tartar Empire stretched from sea to sea, then so would his itinerary. Nothing stands out more impressively than Odoric's austere preparation for missionary life, his tireless wayfaring to reach the scene of his ministry, his return trip for more confriars to bring back to his home in Asia. A man whose face and heart never turned away from Cathay: this is the total description of Odoric's religious career.

And nothing is more evident from his own chronicle, which is practically our only source about his life.

"I desired to travel to the land of the pagans to win the fruit of some souls," he dictated in the first paragraph of his story. In the last paragraph, spoken from the sickbed that later became his deathbed, he said, "Even now from day to day I am preparing to travel to those lands [again], so that I can die there to please Him from Whom comes every good thing."

His spiritual viewpoint is what makes Odoric's narrative different from a travelogue like Marco Polo's. The two longest accounts of Odoric's narrative tell of the Franciscan martyrs of India, whom he longed to imitate, and of the imperial court of Cathay, for the conversion of which he spent his life so generously.

Save for the two foregoing excerpts from his chronicle, Odoric's sanctity never asserts itself. But we can surmise it from the direction of his interests during his travels. He is anxious to describe the religious customs and the moral standards of the people he saw, with an eye to their need for religious enlightenment. Odoric's contemporary, Marco Polo, on the contrary, prefers to enlarge upon the commercial aspects of Eastern travel.

Odoric's knowledge of the Tartars and the grim future possibly in store for him was based on more than the stories current in Europe about their atrocities. We shall have several occasions to insert the testimony and written documents of Odoric's Franciscan confriars.

What is most remarkable about the Franciscan preaching apostolate in Tartary — apart from its outspoken denunciation of Islam, paganism and immorality — is its apologetic tone, its rational defense of Christianity without even the use of Scriptures. Franciscans proverbially stress the Scriptures in their instructions as the real root of Christian belief; yet they were able to accommodate themselves to unbelievers and adopt different tactics.

The best historically founded example of such militant preaching antedates Odoric by half a century. His Franciscan confriar, William Rubruk, who was attending Mangou Khan's court in Karakorum, Tartary, in the year 1254, has left us an account of one of his adventures there.

> Mangou Khan, seeing around him the representatives of various religions, all claiming the truth as their possession, determined on bringing them face to face, and making them explain their various pretensions in the presence of the people. He ordered that a public discussion should take place between the Christians, Mahometans and Buddhists, and even required the ministers of these various creeds to send him in writing a statement of their articles of faith. Rubruk, who was well-informed, eloquent, and of a subtle turn of mind, wished to have a previous understanding with the Nestorians, as to the course they meant to pursue in the discussion. The Nestorians proposed to attack the Mahometans first, and then the idolaters; but the Franciscans opposed this course, alleging that the Mussulmans agreed with Christians as to the unity of God; and this point being granted by them, it was desirable to prove the existence of God to the Bonzes [Buddhist monks], who saw the Divine essence in virtue, perfection, and the soul of each individual being, thus maintaining a system of extensive pantheism. Rubruk, wishing to take measures that should ensure him the victory, proposed to the Nestorians to have a kind of rehearsal, in which he would take the part of Bonzes, and argue against them. But as his adversaries were not very skilful, they were continually worsted in this preparatory exercise; and as they

never brought forward any other proofs than those from Holy
Scripture, Rubruk had to point out to them that these could be
of no avail with men who did not accept the Scriptures. It was,
therefore, decided that Rubruk should speak first, and maintain
the thesis. These things being settled, the meeting took place on
the eve of Pentecost; three of the Emperor's secretaries, a Mus-
sulman, a Buddhist, and a Christian, being appointed as umpires
in the contest. At the opening of the debate, a proclamation by the
Kha-khan [the Great Khan] was read, in which it was forbidden,
under pain of death, that either of the orators should say anything
abusive of their adversaries, or raise any tumult that might stop the
discussion. After the reading of this proclamation, there was a
profound silence in the assembly, to which the most learned men
of each party had been invited; and then the Christians placed
Rubruk in the midst of them, and charged him to maintain their
cause against the pagans. Then a Bonze, who came from China,
rose, and began to speak. "My friend," said he, addressing Rubruk,
"if you find yourself driven to extremity, you would do well to
seek for someone more skilful than yourself."

Rubruk made no answer to this impertinent speech, and the
Chinese continued, "With what wilt thou commence the discussion?
Shall it be on the creation of the world, or on the fate of the soul
after death?"

"Friend," replied the Franciscan, "the questions concerning
those things must not form the beginning of our controversy. All
things come from God — He is the source and origin of whatever
exists; we must, therefore, speak of God first; for we have not the
same ideas concerning the Divinity, and Mangou wishes to know
which of us has the best faith."

The umpires decided that this was reasonable, and Rubruk then
proceeded to prove the existence of God from philosophical argu-
ments; but when he had finished his demonstration, the Chinese
cried:

"One must be mad to think there is but one God! The sages
admit several. Are there not in the world princes of various de-
grees of power, and is not Mangou Khan above them all? It is
the same with the gods. Who is, then, this only God of whom
you speak?"

Then Rubruk replied by enumerating the attributes of the
Divinity and asserting His omnipotence. The Bonze exclaimed and

protested, saying that he could not admit the existence of one omnipotent God.

"If not," said Rubruk, "there is no one among your gods who can with certainty secure you from evil and danger. To what purpose, then, is it to pray to and worship them?"

Finally the Franciscan monk was declared by the umpires, and even by the Chinese Bonze himself, to have gained the victory.[2]

---

2. Huc, l'Abbé E. R., *Christianity in China, Tartary and Tibet* (English translation published by D. and J. Sadlier and Company, New York, 1887; translator not given), Vol. I, pp. 201-204. William Rubruk and his confriar, Bartholomew of Cremona, were sent by King St. Louis of France, a Tertiary Franciscan, to Mangou Khan's court and capital at Karakorum. They left the camp of the Crusaders in Syria on May 7, 1253, and returned to Acre on August 15, 1255. Since Louis was gone when they returned, Rubruk wrote a chronicle to describe what they saw and the results of their mission. The above account is derived from this chronicle. Rubruk describes in greater detail than any medieval traveler the habits of the Tartars, their demands for gifts, their never-ending cruelty. The Tartars had cleared away all traces of town life where they passed, leaving only huge piles of bones as testimonial of their "greatness." Hence the missionaries almost starved to death for want of provisions. Rubruk's relation of Tartar customs, superstitions and religious practices makes his story lively and interesting, as well as important among sociological studies.

CHAPTER 3

Saint and Traveler

 The life of Friar Odoric presents not a few problems for modern biography. We have almost no contemporary references to his activities that tell us more than what is already in his chronicle. Manuscripts in Latin, French, Italian and German attest to the popularity of his own writing directly from the fourteenth century.

He dictated his travelogue, just before he died, at the order of his Provincial Minister, Friar Guidotto of the Paduan Province. As we have mentioned, Odoric rarely reveals his personal holiness in the travelogue; seldom does he permit the reader to glimpse his soul.

It is the spirit of our times to make a saint's life more palpable. His shortcomings and his troubles mean more to us than his asceticism and miracles. Sanctity is more plausible for us if those who achieved it were not unlike ourselves. But Odoric's account is a geographical odyssey, not the spiritual one of the Theresas. A hagiographer has to supplement Odoric's narrative to make it pass for biography.[1]

In any case, Odoric lived toward the end of an era when the saints were practically the only popular and legendary heroes. Most of them ran the same course of hair shirts and the discipline and fasting. And so Odoric. This similarity does not imply that the medieval writers stylized their heroes so as to leave their assertions unreliable; rather, the medieval saints knew the way to God lay ordinarily along the same path — often a monotonous path.

The main problem of Odoric's biography rises from his hidden life. In Italy he lived, a recluse, far from eyes that pry into solitude. He left his retreat only to begin to travel between Italy and China. The fourteen years of his traveling are equally inaccessible, save through his own story and our *post-factum* reasoning and reading between the lines of the text.

---

1. Odoric's own story will always be the prime source for his biographers. Naturally, the present writer has drawn from it as the most authoritative basis for a biography; has, in fact, inserted a few direct quotations — some of them lengthy, since they needed little commentary and enliven Odoric's biography with words from his own pen. Besides, the dialogue which he occasionally injects adds some little drama to a story that would have been less readable had the original text simply been paraphrased.

The Latin text used throughout, especially for the translations, is the *variorum* of Yule-Cordier (Vol. II, Appendix I); their Latin text is largely from a MS in the Bibliothèque Nationale. The present writer, in preparing the translations presented in the following pages, has also consulted the Latin text as published in 1761 in the *Elogio Storico*. See bibliography, page 149.

In general, important place and personal names are given throughout in the forms found most often in the sources which the writer has used. Many of these names have modern variants, but the reader will beyond question be able to recognize them in their older spellings.

When Odoric finally looked upon his native Lombardy once more, death, which had hounded him from Venice to Cambalec and back again, won the last bout in their long struggle together.

The biography of such a man requires more than research into tomes and records. Kings and popes, sultans and khans, routes and customs are just half the story. The other half of Odoric's story was written in his heart, and there we must read it. Even at that we have not lost his personality altogether. The data of his itinerary will yield a spiritual harvest if we garner the facts carefully, sift them and interpret them. The initial caution is always to distinguish between what seems to be the traveler's curiosity and what is the saint's missionary spirit.

St. Francis wrote in his final Rule that only those may be sent abroad who are fit (*idoneos ad mittendum*). St. Bonaventure has explained this passage of the Rule. His words indicate what qualities Odoric's superiors found in him:

A worth-while missionary must desire his office by divine inspiration, not because of light-minded reasons of imprudent judgment. A robust constitution, coupled with an unwavering faith, well-proven virtue and the reputation for irreproachable conduct, completes the list of essential qualities. On the other hand, warns St. Bonaventure, the superiors must beware of releasing those brethren to the mission fields whose main objective is avoiding the daily monotony of conventual discipline.

The lighthearted missionary spirit has been characteristic of the Order from its cradle. The tradition was founded in the gaiety wherewith the Seraphic Father went in 1219 to North Africa to preach and convert the sultan, Melek-el-Kamil. Francis even verified what he preached by daring to undergo ordeal by fire with the sultan's dervishes. The Seraphic Father would deliver his body to the flames along with the holy men of Islam. His religion would be proven true who left the flames unscathed.

The sultan — or the dervishes — refused. But fortified by the sultan's safe-conduct, Francis was off to pray at the Holy Places of Palestine. The authenticity of the legend is manifest from the sultan's gifts to the holy Founder. The ivory horn he gave to Francis is still preserved among the relics of the Patriarchal Basilica in Assisi, under the guardianship of the Friars Minor Conventual for over seven hundred years.

Even while St. Francis walked the dusty roads of Umbria, heaven sanctioned his Fraternity for its missionary efforts. In 1220 the five Protomartyrs of the Order suffered death in Morocco, where Francis had sent them. The five won everlasting glory at the hands of the infidels, and the Order was baptized in their blood.

The Franciscan Order was scarcely a century old when Odoric submitted himself to its authority. The fame of the Friars Minor even then began to rest equally on the twofold pillars of learning and missionary operations. It might be rash to judge whether Hales, Anthony, Bonaventure, Scotus, Bacon or Ockham heads the scholarly group. But it can hardly be challenged that Odoric's place among the early missionary travelers is first.

CHAPTER 4

A Bohemian from Friuli

"Friar Odoric, a Bohemian from Friuli, of the Province of St. Anthony." This is the title Odoric gives himself when he prefaces his travelogue. The "Province of St. Anthony" indicates his religious affiliation as a Friar Minor, a Franciscan. But the "Bohemian from Friuli" needs closer examination to be understood, especially since the Blessed is historically known as Odoric of Pordenone.

Later biographers give his origin as Italian rather than "Bohemian." It goes without saying, of course, that in the Middle Ages one's allegiance was always to a local political unit — a commune, march or duchy — rather than to a country or empire. Odoric can thus be called Italian only by reason of the present extension of the boundaries of that country.

Long before Odoric's birth, Friuli was a part of the Frankish Empire, then of the Holy Roman Empire. The strongest political attachment of the

Friulians, accordingly, lay northward to the Germanic
and Slavic nations, rather than southward to the Latins.[1]
Besides, Ottokar, who received the crown of Bohemia in
1254, ordered a Bohemian garrison stationed in Friuli.
Therefore Odoric might have traced his Bohemian origin
to the extraction of one or both of his parents: some of the
soldiers of the Bohemian garrison undoubtedly took
Friulian women to wife. Odoric was born less than two
decades after the settlement of the foreign garrison in
Friuli, and he could easily have been the offspring of
such a union.[2]

Friuli belonged to the district within the Patriarchate
of Aquileia, and had once been subordinate to this city
in ecclesiastical jurisdiction. In relation to the Franciscan
Order, at the end of the thirteenth century, Friuli was one
of the four custodies (subdivisions) of the Province of
St. Anthony of Padua.[3]

Nevertheless, despite this accent on Friuli, Odoric's
eulogy in the Martyrology calls him "of Pordenone."
This is an Italian corruption of Port Naon, a district of
Friuli. It was given the exalted title of "Port" because
it lies on a waterway, a tributary of the Livenza River.

---

1. From the ethnical point of view, the Lombards of North Italy are
aligned with the French and Germans. This is largely a result of the
incursions, from the fifth to the tenth centuries A. D., of the Teutonic
peoples as invaders, mercenaries or settlers. The racial similarity between
Italians of the South, Sicilians (*Magna Graecia*) and Greeks is due mainly
to the colonization from the seventh to the fourth centuries B. C.

2. *Elogio Storico,* pp. 2 and 3. See also the chart of Ottokar's
genealogical tree, facing p. 2. The name Friuli, incidentally, is a corruption of the two Latin words *Forum Julii.*

3. The other three were the Paduan Custody, the Venetian Custody
and the Veronese Custody. Thus Odoric's province included several important Italian towns.

Even if it was important enough in Roman times to have merited the title of "Port," although it is not a sea harbor, nevertheless in medieval times it was dwarfed by the huge shipping port of Venice nearby.

Pordenone has thus given its own name to its famous son, to replace his family name, Matthiussi.

The baptismal name of Odoric was either in token of St. *Uldaric,* Bishop and Confessor, the patron of the local parish church; or in memory of *Udalric* II, Duke of Carinthia, of Ottokar's family, who would have succeeded to the lordship of Pordenone had he not died. In any case, Odoric — or the foregoing variations — was a common name in those parts at that time.

The year of salvation 1285 is best assigned as the friar's birth date. Rudolph I of Hapsburg reigned in the Holy Roman Empire, and James Savelli, Honorius IV, sat in Peter's chair. The Franciscan Order was just seventy-six years old.

Odoric was only four or five years old when news reached Rome that was significantly to affect the whole course of his later religious life. In 1289 the message was carried from faraway Tartary to the Franciscan Pope, Nicholas IV. Unlike previous reports from out of the obscure realms of Tartary, this message was enthusiastically worded. There was an uncounted multitude of men, it read, who had already entered the one fold of Christ out in Tartary. The fields were proverbially white for the harvest of souls; men thirsted for the word of God. Even where the rulers were not amenable to the faith, at least they did not impede missionary labors.

Pope Nicholas did not let his opportunity slip past without action. The new Tartar policy — especially in Cathay — that favored "foreign" culture and ideas deserved the fullest exploitation for the sake of Christ and souls. He wrote at once to Prince Caydo of Turkistan, to King Argon of Persia, and to Cobyla Khan of Cathay — the last-named of whom history has transformed into the more familiar Kublai Khan. . . .

To Cobyla Khan, the illustrious great Leader of the Tartars, grace in the present life, which may lead to glory in the future life. We rejoice in the Lord, noble Prince, and extend to you Our manifold, sincere thanks. We are happy to have heard that He Who holds the hearts of earthly rulers in His hand has fixed deeply within your heart by the merciful gift of His grace the desire of increasing the boundaries of Christianity. Some time after We began the negotiations, We admitted some legates to Our presence, sent by that generous Prince, the illustrious King Argon of Tartary. The legates openly told Us of the deep devotion Your Highness bears for Our Person, the Roman Church, and the nations of the West. The legates were quite insistent in behalf of their royal master that We send some Western teachers [*religiosos latinos*] to your court. We were exceedingly joyful in the Lord to hear such a report about so great and sublime a Prince, because We sincerely desire your increase in merit and the glory of your name. We humbly beg the Father of Light, from Whom is every best and perfect gift, to enlighten your inmost heart that you may always progress from good to better by reason of His inspiration. May He shed the dew of His grace on you for the praise and honor of His glorious name. We therefore wish kindly to acquiesce to the royal petition; We desire you to embrace the Christian faith which is taught and preserved by the Roman Church. Come forth promptly, offer yourself openly, anxiously hasten, because no one can please the Most High without His aid. We are sending you Our beloved son Friar John of Monte Corvino, and his Franciscan confriars, who will bear this letter to you. We ask that you receive him and his companions with kindness. We hope that you adhere to their teaching as the hope of your salvation moves you. Give them the help of your royal favor in this business entrusted to them, which concerns the salvation of souls. Leaning on such a support, they will acquit themselves more ably and efficaciously of their assignment; and you, on the other hand, will receive the reward of eternal blessedness from the Lord, Who repays manifold times for the least good. Given at Reate, on the third day before the Ides of July, in the second year of Our reign [1289].[4]

---

4. Translated from Luke Wadding, *Annales Minorum* (Quaracchi, 1931-1932), Vol. V, p. 219. Actually, Kublai Khan never had any intention of turning Christian, although it is more than possible that he gave material assent to being baptized without ever having formally consented to accept the teaching of the Church. He was notably tolerant of all religions, according to the policy of his predecessor Genghis Khan, real founder of the Mongol Dynasty. It was generally the Moslem Tartars, further west in the empire, who were so hostile to Christians. The John of Monte Corvino mentioned by Nicholas IV is the one who subsequently became the first Archbishop of Cambalec (later, Peking, which in modern times is known by still another name: Peiping). Odoric will speak of him in his chronicle.

CHAPTER 5

"Let Him Deny Himself ... "

 The letter of Pope Nicholas IV to Kublai Khan began a long series of friendly interchanges between the papacy and the imperial court of Cathay. The other temporal rulers' chief concern was to augment their territories; the popes looked to spiritual empires waiting for conquest across land and sea.

Nevertheless, the fear of the Tartars was still a paramount threat to all of Europe. By this time Tartars of Cathay, however thin their veneer of civilization, had very little in common with their more violent brethren who dwelt in the lands between Siberia and the Black Sea. There was always the anxiety in the West that the barbarians would ride once more against the puny princes of Europe. But the anxiety that had a greater influence on Odoric's life was the fear felt by the popes that these wild children of the tundras would be lost to their spiritual jurisdiction.

But God was bending out of heaven, making plans of His own to vanquish Tartar souls and tame their stubborn hearts for Himself. He watched a young Lombard grow into adolescence. He was impatient to whisper His pleasure into the boy's ear. Because of Odoric's military heritage — he was the son of a Bohemian soldier family — tales of the Tartars must have stirred him and made him eager to be off to investigate their bravery for himself. His chronicle gives us to believe that he never lost this boyish curiosity; he was to consider it nothing at all to add a few hundred miles on land and countless leagues across the sea to investigate the curiosities he heard about or stumbled upon.

It was 1300. The thirteenth century of saints and philosophers was over. The Renaissance was beginning and Odoric had just turned fifteen. Either because the medievals were short-lived or because they shared family responsibility earlier than nowadays, fifteen years represented a young man's majority. Odoric chose his career.

His soldier ancestry must have beckoned to him and offered martial glory in danger and the adventures of camping and outdoor life. Nor was such a destiny denied him by the God Who had claimed Odoric for His own, signing him with the seal of a chosen soul. Indeed, Odoric had many times over his share of danger, camping under the open sky and enduring the rigors of the march. He had a portion of all of these — several thousand miles' worth.

One day the fifteen-year-old pulled the doorbell of the Franciscan friary in nearby Udine. His request to begin his novitiate was not refused. He exchanged his

doublet for a gray tunic of undyed wool, his leather boots
for rough sandals, his wide belt for a rope around his
waist. Most of all, he exchanged the world for its Creator.
The sincerity of Odoric's exchange was without doubt
tested by God and superior. But we can surmise that he
did not turn to look back, once he set himself to plow
a straight furrow direct to the horizons of heaven. After a
year Odoric placed his hands within his superior's over a
Book of the Gospels and told the Trinity, the Virgin,
Michael the Archangel, and Peter and Paul, that his mind
was made up to live in obedience, without property and
in chastity.

After pronouncing this formula of profession, Odoric
began his studies for the priesthood. If he applied himself diligently to philosophy and theology, then it was
only, an early biography relates, to have more time free
for the sacred writers and the book of the cross of
Christ. His meat and drink was the Rule of St. Francis
and the Constitutions of Narbonne, promulgated almost
half a century earlier by St. Bonaventure, the Minister
General. The Rule and Constitutions are the norm of
sanctity for a community, the common and ordinary way
of being busy about perfection. But the ordinary and
common way is just a springboard for the saints.

We have already said that Odoric's self-discipline
reads like the accounts of saints of bygone days. This of
course gives us no right to infer that his austerity is a
fiction of his too pious but not too accurate biographer.
It is rather that we who are given to self-indulgence are
slow to concede such heroism in others. Actually Odoric's
abnegation was the best preparation he could have made

for his future career. His refusal, for example, to wear heavier clothes in winter or lighter clothes in summer inured his body alike to the torrid zone of the East Indies and to the frostbitten plains of central Russia and Tibet. In addition, his frequent bread-and-water fasts were not wholly unlike the frugal Tartar diet of barley cakes and fermented mare's milk.

Even such a degree of mortification was not enough. To goad, prick and spur himself to think of heaven, Odoric used a time-proven device on his body: small plates of cold metal linked about his waist next to his skin and an iron chain bound tightly around each arm. Thus his habit concealed iron ornaments of which the gold and silver belts and bracelets were the world's counterpart. You may feel some disbelief; Odoric felt the pain.

In fact, we might be surprised at the number of hair shirts and disciplines worn out and used up even today. The point to remember is that Odoric did not *enjoy* the pain. This would have both made him a sadist and made his pleasure deserving of condemnation — to say nothing of the accusation of modern psychiatry. No, Odoric did not enjoy the bodily burden of links and chains cutting into his flesh to remind him, at every step, that he could not even move without God. But their being a bodily burden is the best reason for a saint to wear chains. We might add that a lack of such mortification is often the very reason why some modern missionaries have little success in converting the pagans of the East: Oriental bonzes, fakirs and holy men practice austerity to an appalling degree that Westerners do not even attempt to imitate. True, mortification is only an external adjunct to the spiritual life, but nonetheless it is morally necessary: there is nothing that happens in the body that does not have a proportionate good or bad effect on the soul, too.

To Odoric's chagrin, his confriars tried to make a superior of him. His preoccupation with God attracted scores of the laity, especially when he sat in the confessional or stood in the pulpit. We read that his gift of curing sickness even so early in his life made him the object of pious veneration. A state of affairs so distasteful to Odoric was only God's mysterious plan of packing Odoric off to Tartary. His conscience directed him to escape this desire on the part of others to become his subjects and admirers. He asked leave to prepare for the missions.

The preparation was first of all interior. Odoric fled to a hermitage for several months to gather up a treasure of divine graces to take with him to Tartary. The external preparation was almost nothing. The *Breviarium Romano-Seraphicum,* in the Office of Blessed Odoric, says he made no provision for his travels but depended, for thousands of miles through hostile lands and among barbaric peoples, on the immediate, day-by-day providence of God. Our Lord says something about no staff, no scrip, and no money. Yet the little biography in the Breviary says God never failed him — even at times feeding and sustaining him miraculously. And for the refreshment of his soul on his travels, the Virgin Mother and other saints visited him in Persia, India, China, Tartary, to console him with words of his heavenly fatherland, for the sake of which he had left his earthly country.

Even during Odoric's time of preparation in his mountain recess the faithful could not be kept from their spiritual father. Men who needed faith found him out. Tepid souls reclaimed their hope through him. And to the souls who fed on love, Odoric preached the same habit he himself wore.

Finally one day Blessed Odoric came off his mountain and with a smile of satisfaction turned his face toward Cathay.

CHAPTER 6

Farewell to Italy

Odoric's travelogue begins at this point of his life. It is 1316.[1] The friar was just thirty when he embarked on the voyage to Cathay that won him the reputation of being the Franciscan Marco Polo. He had already spent about fifteen years of his thirty in the Minorite Order of St. Francis.

Venice was his port of embarkation. Even if Odoric had not so written, we could easily have surmised the fact. Venice was the closest port of note to Udine — and without doubt the chief port of Europe in the trade with the Orient. Since Odoric's destination was Asia Minor, he left in a vessel powered both by oar and by sail. Galleys driven by oarsmen alone, were the means of transportation only on short runs — especially if the traveling

---

1. Some authorities hold out for 1318. But this would make Odoric's travels of only twelve years' duration, whereas reliable MSS expressly mention some fourteen and a half years abroad. We are certain of the date of his return, 1330.

was coastwise and not across the open sea. How Odoric secured passage in the first place is nowhere evident. It is a fair guess that the friar who never made provision for the future had to beg his way on board. Some benefactor might have paid his way, or some kind merchant might have chartered his passage either as part of the ship's cargo or as the saintly guarantee of the ship's safety, if the merchant himself were voyaging with his cargo. After all, piracy was no uncommon means of livelihood in those days, either for Christian or for Moslem.

Perhaps the most probable answer of all is that a special agency helped him out. In 1252 Pope Innocent IV approved a group called the Society of Pilgrims for the Sake of Christ. This was an organization of Dominicans and Franciscans dedicated to foreign missionary service. Odoric could profit by what they told him of the places he had to visit and how to go about getting there alive. This society could have supplied him with letters of introduction and words of advice on itineraries, customs and language.

Regardless of how he got passage aboard the Venetian galley, we can be sure that Odoric slept on deck with the crew and ordinary passengers. Privacy was not a part of medieval life anyway. Besides, cabins were a rarity and reserved solely for a wealthy or noble clientele. There were no passenger boats as such, only cargo ships.

A ship bound out of Venice for the opposite end of the Mediterranean ordinarily set sail in spring to take advantage of the weather. Odoric's vessel probably

weighed anchor in April. What will always remain a
mystery is whether or not the friar had any companion.[2]
All this time he wore the habit of his Order — which must
have appeared quite outlandish to the Asiatics, not to
mention unduly heavy for tropic climes. Since Odoric
was able to stay at least at a few friaries of the Order
during his travels, he could easily have obtained a re-
placement during the fourteen years of travel, if the old
habit would no longer bear repatching.

It is not difficult to imagine how Odoric used his time
on the voyage out of Venice. There was the daily round
of canonical hours he was obliged to recite according to
the custom of the Roman Church, plus the usual time to
be spent in prayer and meditation. We can be sure that
the friar did not miss the chance to learn and practice the
languages that would serve him well in the near future.
Latin was, of course, the *koine,* or common tongue, of
the West; Greek was the language of traders in the
Mediterranean basin and in the Near East. To get along
in the Middle and Far East, the only language needed was
Arabic, which had received great currency after the seventh
century from the militant spread of Islam, its rich culture

2. Yule (bibliography, p. 150) says that a Friar James of Ireland
may have accompanied Odoric on part of his journey. This he deduces
from a gift made by Udine on April 5, 1331, to a Friar James, "the
companion of Blessed Odoric." But it appears doubtful to the present
writer that this James would have been with him for any length of time
on his travels without Odoric's mentioning the friar by name in his
chronicle. Besides, the gift was made after Odoric's death and long after
his return to Italy. This Friar James may have been Odoric's companion
only during his final sickness. Nevertheless, Odoric does refer to a
companion in India, although he does not say whether the companion was
another Franciscan, much less mention him by name. Elsewhere Odoric
uses the first person singular in his narrative, save for the mention of
a servant or of other travelers.

and opulent trade.[3] To use the words of Odoric, already in India, he was able to speak "Armorice," or "Armenice," that is, the tongue used by the Armenians. Nevertheless, the latter term was general enough to include practically any language spoken by these well-known traders from south of the Caucasus and along the caravan routes from the Black Sea to the Caspian.

The ship carrying Odoric made its slow way down the Adriatic Sea, hugging the coast of Dalmatia or Italy. Then around the Peloponnesus of Greece and through the countless islands scattered between modern Greece and Turkey. Finally, Constantinople, or Istanbul, filled their horizon; disembarkation was near at hand.

Next they navigated the Black Sea, which the ancients called the Euxine, and which Odoric called the Greater Sea and bottomless. Up to this point Odoric has said nothing of his passage. As he himself asserts in the opening lines of his travelogue, his purpose is to relate the wonders of the East, especially such as have not been recorded before.

When Odoric disembarked and said farewell to the men who had been his companions on the tedious voyage

---

3. There were possibly hundreds of friars in Odoric's time from nearby Spain, North Africa and Sicily who could have given him lessons in Arabic. Mohammedan attacks, or at least trading ventures, established easy contact with Arabic and other languages. Moreover, the renowned Spanish Franciscan mystic, Blessed Ramón Lull, had founded a missionary college in 1276 at Majorca, Spain, for the purpose of studying the language and habits and philosophy of the "Arabians" — that is, the Mohammedans. Although this college was of only twenty years' duration, it shows the Franciscans' experience in linguistics. In further illustration is the fact that, a few years before Odoric's departure from Italy, in 1303, some German Franciscans actually compiled a lexicon of one species of the Tartar language, under the title *Codex Cumanicus*.

from Venice, he knew he was in a city of Asia. The name of this city was Trebizond, and it was located on the southern coast of the Black Sea, as the map indicates. Trebizond was an important trading station at this time, because the Crusades had closed off access to the East through the towns lying further south. In Old Testament times the region was known as Tubal; when Odoric landed there, the district was called the empire of Trebizond under Alexius II.

Odoric did not tarry in Trebizond, but hurried south into Greater Armenia. The country grows mountainous directly away from the sea. As he passed through to Erzerum — a city of modern Turkey and the principal city of the Turkomans in Odoric's day — the friar noted the high altitude and extreme cold.

Going deeper and deeper into Armenia, Odoric soon passed under the shadow of Mount Ararat. This is the peak which tradition claims as the resting place of Noe's ark after the flood receded. It was a sacred place to the local people and even forbidden. Odoric badly wanted to climb the snow-covered Ararat in this wintry climate — once more the boy's love of adventure and curiosities — but the group with which he was traveling refused to wait. Evidently the friar had attached himself to some caravan whose direction was his own. It was a common thing for merchants and travelers of all kinds to band together for protection against raiders who lived by plundering unwary travelers and unprotected caravans. They would all have been en route to the next town Odoric describes, the fabulous Tabriz.

CHAPTER 7

Persian Days and Nights

 Tabriz is a corruption of the older name of Tauris. It was the most important city of Persia in Odoric's time. Actually, Persia was only one division of the Tartar Empire, and the Tartar Empire was a loose confederation of Tartar people and the nations they conquered. Even though every province owed some kind of allegiance to the Great Khan of Cathay, to whom Odoric was making his way, each lesser khan ruled the way he chose.

The strategic central location of Tabriz had contrived to keep it an important city for about two thousand years before the thirteenth century. It lay on the trade route coming out of north central Asia into Asia Minor and Europe. Tabriz was a key city both of the ancient Persians and of the Seleucid monarchs who succeeded Alexander the Great. It remained a key city under Roman domination, and Greek and Arab and Tartar domination, too.

Tabriz must have impressed Odoric immensely. Like most Europeans — even today — Odoric probably thought of the East as uncivilized and barbaric. After all, he was taking Christianity to them, so they could not have been very civilized, Odoric may have reasoned. That is why the superiority of Tabriz over any European town he could have visited was a surprise. Tabriz may very well have been the largest city in the world at that time, numbering a million and a quarter inhabitants. Odoric uses superlatives of several cities in which he tarried, so it is not always clear which was the greatest city either in fact or in his own mind.

The pre-eminence of Tabriz during Odoric's visit is understandable for another reason. Shortly before his arrival, Baghdad had been destroyed by Hulagu Khan. Its extensive trade had therefore been diverted into Tabriz. In addition, Tabriz lay north of and further away from the constant warfare between Christian and Saracen in the eastern Mediterranean area. Tabriz might thus easily be labeled the meeting place between East and West — especially in the economic sense. It was a huge, overflowing market place.

"This city," Odoric wrote, "is more noble and better for trade today than any other the world over. There is no edible thing, nor anything that has market value, of which there is not a great abundance in Tabriz. It is such a marvelous city that you would scarcely believe what you find there. The reason is that the city itself has such an advantageous location: practically the whole world conducts business with Tabriz. Christians are wont to say that the emperor of Persia receives more from the traffic of this one city than the king of France has from his entire kingdom."

Despite the Oriental environment, Odoric was at home in Tabriz. We know of at least two convents of the Order there, so he had the companionship of his own brethren for a little while longer. We know of these establishments because the Dominican Jordanus addressed a letter to the brethren there on October 12, 1321 — or shortly after Odoric passed through.

The friar mentions that Christians of all kinds (*cuiuslibet generationis*) were living in the city. This indicates not only the Greek Catholics, but the Nestorian Christians, whom Odoric was to meet many times on his travels. We shall have cause to mention the Nestorian heretics again with reference to the Franciscan Archbishop of Cambalec. For the most part, of course, Islam was the religion of the people of Persia, from the region under the Black Sea down to Ormuz on the Persian Gulf. Odoric always calls a Moslem by the name of Saracen, even as far east as China itself, because most Europeans connected Islam with the Saracens, with whom the Crusaders in Palestine and Egypt did most of their battling.

From Tabriz the friar hurried southeast along the caravan trails for ten days through the mountains till he reached the city of Soltania — the summer residence of the Tartar khans in Persia. This was a comparatively new city, built at least in part just a few years before Odoric entered its gates. Like Tabriz, although not on nearly so large a scale, Soltania was a market place for merchandise of all kinds.

As in Tabriz, Odoric found another house of the Order
in Soltania. He could have stayed either with his own
confriars or with the Dominicans. Pope John XXII had
appointed a Friar Preacher — thus the Dominicans were
designated — as the archbishop in Soltania before 1318.
This is approximately the time Odoric passed through.
The need for an archbishopric in the district openly attests
to the fruitful preaching of Dominican and Franciscan
friars. It was as if the two infant Orders were joyously
emulating each other in the Asiatic apostolate, in imitation
of the happy friendship of the two holy founders, Dominic
Guzmán and Francis Bernardone.

Odoric left Soltania as a member of a caravan (*cum
caravanis*) which skirted the mountain range that crowds
south of the Caspian Sea, which was called the Sea of
Bacuc at that time. The friar was still following the
ancient overland trade route which led from the Black to
the Arabian Sea. Before the Christian-Islamic wars, these
overland caravan routes down to the Indian waters were
less important and less traveled. Had it not been for the
perils of the wars throughout Syria, Palestine and Egypt,
merchandise could have been passed more quickly and
more cheaply by the water route from Alexandria, Egypt,
to the Red Sea, and out into the Indian Ocean.

In few words Odoric narrated how he passed through
Kashan, which was the alleged starting point of the Magi
thirteen centuries earlier. From Kashan, still moving
toward the place where the southeastern end of the Persian
Empire met the northwestern end of Upper India, our
friar traveled through Ispahan to Yezd, a prosperous town
at the edge of the legendary Sea of Sand. (See map.)

Travelers did not dare to cross this Sea of Sand (*Mare Arenosum*), not even the wealth seekers who were trying to reach the rich provinces of Kashmir and the Punjab, which lay on the other side. To paraphrase Odoric's chronicle, this desert had, and still has, waves of shifting sands. It was fairly impossible to lay any roads or mark any routes of travel. The few adventurers who hazarded the journey commonly lost their lives in the dry wastelands. Sandstorms and hot winds contrived to suffocate and bury alive the foolhardy traveler.

From Yezd, Friar Odoric continued ever southward through several towns till he reached Comerum, or Conium. This was the ancient Persepolis, famous in classical stories as the treasure house of the Persian kings, whom Alexander the Great conquered in his march to the Indus River. The young Macedonian actually unbalanced the Mediterranean world's economy for many decades by pouring out all at once the treasure-troves of Cyrus, Darius and Xerxes. The city of Comerum lay in ruins when the friar passed by. Animals were its only citizens. Nevertheless Odoric noted that several of the larger buildings (*palacia*) were still intact and habitable.

At this stage of his overland journey to the Arabian Sea, Friar Odoric halts his southward progress and practically reverses his direction. He includes on his itinerary, for some reason he does not mention, the land of Job, the city of Hus in the Old Testament, and Chaldea. Although this excursus has no apparent explanation, perhaps the boy's curiosity had welled up again. Besides, there may have been no ships out of Arabian ports this time of year, and Odoric may have wanted to reconnoiter the territory for possible missionary exploration, in order to spend his time profitably for his Order. Perhaps he desired to visit in person the many places he had read about in the Old Testament.

Whatever his reason, Odoric wandered in the direction of ancient Babylon and of medieval Baghdad, recently destroyed, as we noted above, by Hulagu Khan, the Tartar general sent forth by Genghis Khan. The friar passed by the ruins of what he supposed was the Tower of Babel. We can be sure he stopped for a meditation on the emptiness of human pride, the futility of Godless endeavors.

Odoric has left a description of the condition of Moslem women in ancient Chaldea, not neglecting a few remarks about the men, too:

"The men are handsome [*pulchri*], but the women are slovenly [*turpes*]. The men go around with their hair dressed and wearing jewelry [*compti et ornati*], as do the women of our own land. They wear a headband of gold set with pearls.

"The women wear a single tunic reaching to their knees. Its sleeves are so long and ample that they touch the ground. The women walk about barefoot, and with pantaloons [*sarabulas*] of ankle length. Their hair is neither parted nor worn in braids, but left to hang unkemptly on all sides [*capilli undique disparguntur*].

"Men in our country allow their women to precede them; there, in Chaldea, the men walk ahead of the women."

Friar Odoric turned back in his original direction and headed southeast once again. His next stop — and the last city of Persia he was to see for a dozen years — was Ormuz. Marco Polo relates in his travelogue that the road to Ormuz descends rapidly to the sea. The way was beset by robbers who preyed on the heavily laden caravans moving down to Ormuz to unload their wares to be transferred aboard merchant vessels bound for India, the East Indian Islands and China.

The city of Ormuz was located astride a tiny island about five miles offshore at the point where the narrowing Persian Gulf empties into the Arabian Sea and ultimately into the Indian Ocean. It was transferred from the shore to the island by one of its previous rulers, in order to safeguard the wealth of the city against robber attacks. The city was well fortified on its island. One is immediately reminded of ancient Tyre off the coast of Phoenicia. That city was likewise built on a spit of sand a small distance offshore for the sake of protection. Young Alexander swore to take Tyre. With great effort and loss of life — nearly his own — Alexander had a causeway built out to the city, where his engines of war could be trained effectively against Tyre's high and massive stone walls.

Ormuz, off the coast of Persia, was like Tyre not only in its key location, but also in its maritime occupation. It lay midway between all the overseas trade of India and China, and such merchandise centers as Baghdad, Tabriz and Trebizond, not excluding the ports of Constantinople and faraway Venice. We read of Venetian merchants living and trading in practically every city through which

Odoric passed on his mission to Cathay. It is quite evident that Odoric adhered closely to the trade routes overland and the sea lanes of commerce. It is a safe conclusion that his own countrymen helped him to make his tedious way from town to town.

Ibn Batuta, a Mohammedan chronicler and traveler who flourished shortly after Odoric's own time, wrote that the city of Ormuz was on a barren island. Its only natural resource was the rock salt it exported in abundance. But as an emporium it rivaled all the great seaports of the world. Indian traders in particular made Ormuz the outlet for their gems, spices and ivory.

Perhaps the most unusual characteristic of Ormuz was neither its unique location nor its prominence as a trading station between the Near and the Middle East. Its peculiar weather is what generally interests the reader most. The heat is unbearably intense — at least so a few medieval travelers described it.

Marco Polo wrote of the offshore wind that blew in the late morning. Evidently it came from the desert, the Sea of Sand, which we have named above as the barrier to a possible land route to the northern parts of India. (See map.) In the worst heat of summer, wrote Friar Odoric, citizens of Ormuz left their hot and barren island in favor of their gardens on the mainland. They sought refuge from the searing heat especially along the banks of the river which emptied into the Persian Gulf opposite Ormuz. They constructed shelters, half in the river and half on its bank. These they made of wickerwork and covered with broad leaves. During the suffocating heat that was brought on the face of the wind from the sandy desert, the inhabitants stayed in the water up to their chins — so the account goes.

Once it happened that the ruler of Kierman, to whom Ormuz owed tribute, sent an army to the city when most of the citizens were in their summer shelters during the heat waves. When the army of Kierman was overtaken by this wind — they evidently did not reckon its heat so suffocating — they perished to a man. The entire contingent of 1,600 cavalry and 5,000 infantry, Marco Polo tells us, was suffocated in a matter of hours. The fact that Marco Polo says he was in Ormuz when this extraordinary event occurred, lends some weight to his claims.

Polo's final remark is that the people of Ormuz had to dig the graves for the putrefying corpses where they had fallen. The severe sun and wind had dried and baked their bodies so thoroughly that the limbs fell from the torso when they were being handled — like those of an overdone fowl. So much for Marco Polo. It is easier to believe his story when we remember that Blessed Odoric's story of the heat of Ormuz seems at first reading no less incredible.

CHAPTER 8

Passage to India

⊚⊚⊚⊚⊚⊚⊚⊚⊚⊚⊚⊚⊚⊚⊚⊚⊚⊚⊚⊚⊚⊚⊚⊚⊚⊚⊚⊚⊚⊚⊚⊚⊚⊚

Finally Odoric secured passage to India and took ship out of Ormuz. If it was summer when he stayed in that city, the friar must have thought it at least incongruous to crouch a couple of hours during the midday heat, up to his neck in water in a shelter built on a Persian riverbank. It was not the worst thing he endured during his travels, but the ocean voyage must have been refreshing anyway.

Odoric is heartily in accord with other medieval opinions on the negative seaworthiness of the vessels that plied between Ormuz and India. Marco Polo, the Dominican Jordanus, and the Franciscan John of Monte Corvino join Odoric in amazed criticism of these ships. Odoric himself says he could not find iron used anywhere in their construction, neither nails nor braces. Nails could not even be driven into the hard wood of which the ships were built; or if they were driven in, the boards split.

Instead, the shipwrights used wooden pegs. Odoric wrote that the boats were *stitched* together with twine. Marco Polo mentions that they were sewn together with a kind of rope woven of fibers from the husks of the large Indian nut. Perhaps the boards were laced together by fastening the twine from peg to peg. No one's explanation is completely satisfactory.

The shipbuilders substituted rather thin fish oil for the better preservative of pitch and resin. Small wonder, then, that the storms over the west coast of the Indian peninsula took a large toll of vessels, merchandise and lives. Only the insatiable desire for wealth could have driven human beings to undertake perilous voyages in such craft — that or else the insatiable desire for souls.

Friar Odoric made the voyage from Ormuz in the Persian Gulf to Tana, India, in twenty-eight days. Tana had a location analogous to Ormuz on its island, lying offshore on the island named Salsette. The city was the capital of the whole coastal region from the Rajput States down to Malabar; this coastal region was known as Konkan. (See map.)

As the map indicates, India was not part of the conquered domain of the Tartars. Its strong native rulers and the natural boundaries of the ocean and the Himalaya mountain chain protected it from invasion. Such was the militant spirit of Islam that whole sections of the Konkan coastal district were of the Mohammedan persuasion, some even for centuries. Although the *rulers* of the island of Salsette were followers of Islam, the bulk of the *inhabitants* were idolaters. They worshiped snakes, trees and fire. The Moslems — or Saracens, as Odoric is wont to say — conquered the region and subjected it to the empire of the sultans of Delhi.

Regardless, however, of the organized rule of the mainland, voyagers like Odoric and his companions had to keep a careful eye out for pirates. Marco Polo gives us an interesting account of piracy in Indian waters and their clever mode of operation:

> In this country [Malabar] the north star is seen about two fathoms above the horizon. Here as in the kingdom of Guzerat, which is not far distant, there are numerous pirates, who yearly scour these seas with more than one hundred small vessels, seizing and plundering all the merchant ships that pass that way. They take with them to sea their wives and children of all ages, who continue to accompany them during the whole of the summer's cruise. In order that no ships may escape them, they anchor their vessels at the distance of five miles from each other; twenty ships occupy a space of a hundred miles. Upon a trader's appearing in sight of one of them, a signal is made by fire or smoke; when they draw closer together, and capture the vessel as she attempts to pass. No injury is done to the crew, but as soon as they have made prize of the ship, they turn them on shore, recommending to them to provide themselves with another cargo, which, in case of their passing that way again, may be the means of enriching their captors a second time.... [Guzerat also] affords harbour to pirates of the most desperate character. When in their cruises they seize upon a traveling merchant they immediately oblige him to drink a dose of seawater which produces violent purging. In this way they discover whether he has swallowed pearls or jewels.[1]

For the hagiographer, the most important matter in connection with Odoric's stay in Tana is not the boat he used to get there, nor the location and exports of the

---

1. Quoted by permission of the Liveright Publishing Corporation, New York, from pp. 299-301 of *The Travels of Marco Polo,* revised from Marsden's translation and edited with an introduction by Manuel Komroff; $2.98. Copyright R 1953 by Manuel Komroff.

city, nor even the pirates that threatened the shipping. We are interested in the four Franciscan martyrs of Tana, who won their crown shortly before Odoric's arrival. He relates their story in great detail.[2]

The next two chapters (9 and 10) are translated from the Franciscan historian Luke Wadding, who gives us a more complete account of the suffering of the four martyrs and includes other sources besides Odoric's narrative. That we should devote two entire chapters to the martyrs of Tana is warranted by the length of the narrative dictated by Odoric himself, as well as by the interest intrinsic to the story as found in both Wadding's and Odoric's chronicles.[3]

---

2. Odoric probably stayed in Tana with the Dominican missionary Jordanus, whom we have mentioned elsewhere. We know of the Dominican's presence in this city through a letter of 1323 — written soon after Odoric's arrival in Tana and addressed to all Dominican and Franciscan missionaries in the Orient — dealing with the martyrdom of the four Franciscans. The account of his own longing for a martyr's crown and his grief at being left by God on earth while he saw his Franciscan companions tortured, is among the most beautiful passages of the letter of the holy Jordanus.

3. The entire selection given in chapters 9 and 10 has been translated by the author from Wadding's *Annales Minorum,* Vol. VI, pp. 309 sqq. For the sake of easier reading, the text is not set within quotation marks except where such internal punctuation appears with the dialogue.

CHAPTER 9

Luke Wadding's Account
of the Martyrs of Tana

In this year [1321] on April 9, which was the Thursday before Palm Sunday, four illustrious champions of the faith, members of the Franciscan Order, suffered a glorious martyrdom. They were Friars Thomas of Tolentino, whom we have often mentioned in these annals — now he was sixty years old — and James of Padua, of the Province of St. Anthony, Peter of Siena, of the Tuscan Province, and Demetrius, a lay brother of Tiflis, a Georgian by birth. This Demetrius acted as interpreter for the friars, since he was so clever in the Oriental tongues. . . .

It is only fitting to tell the story of how in our own day the grace of God, our Savior Jesus Christ, has been made manifest in His servants. According to the prophecy of Zacharias [6:2], a chariot has come forth, drawn by four ruddy and robust steeds, who have run their course over the whole earth.

Like the four winds have they burst forth to stand before
the Lord of the whole earth. . . . [1]

The Nestorian Christian at whose house in Tana the
friars were staying, maltreated his wife. She took her
complaint to the Cadi [the Mohammedan priest], who
handled affairs pertaining to the Mohammedan religion.
As witness of the injuries done to her, she named the four
men from the West who were living at her home [*hospites
latinos*]. The friars were called to testify — unwillingly,
not knowing what to say. At the instigation of a certain
man of Alexandria named Oseph, they were sent to the
governor of the city [*urbis praetorem*].[2] This Alexandrian
hated people from the West and left nothing undone to
have the governor deal harshly with the friars.

The governor, however, was of a milder disposition,
and after questioning them about the faith, the books of
the Bible they were carrying with them, and their travels,
he sent them away in peace. But the Alexandrian used
both fraud and malice to have them recalled a third
and a fourth time. Finally, this question was put to them
before the Cadi: How did they compare the Moslem and
Christian religions?

The friars fearlessly responded that Islam was the
way of perdition and Mohammed was a worthless wretch
and a damnable faker, whereas Christianity was the way of

---

1. A metaphorical reference to the four martyrs, ruddy in their own
blood, yet robust in the faith, who had traveled all over the known
world of their day. It was Thomas of Tolentino's third visit to the Orient.
2. He is named Mellichus in Wadding's *Annales,* but this is rather
the title of his office, made into a proper name. In other sources, as
well as in some Oriental languages, the root contained in *Melek* or *Melik*
appears as the title of some local dignitary, or even of a sultan or king.

salvation and Christ was the Son of God and true God Himself.

The Cadi was enraged by this reply. He threatened to kill them unless they retracted their words against Mohammed, the great prophet and messenger of God. When they refused, he changed his threats to bribes and offered these soldiers of Christ gifts to soften them. But the friars were not afraid of threats nor turned by gifts.

Meanwhile the Mohammedans cried out, demanding their death. At last they rushed against the friars in a mob, dragged them from their place of worship, and tied them with bared heads to posts. They intended that the brethren should suffer a stroke and die in the burning sun of India. At that time of the year a person's exposure to the sun for one full hour could result in his death. But the four friars remained in the broiling sun from the third to the ninth hour of the day, glorifying and praising God, Who miraculously mitigated the fierce rays of the sun and caused a pleasant breeze to blow about them.

The amazed Mohammedans next led them to the governor and Cadi and tried every means of getting the Franciscans to accept Islam. When this availed nothing, they lit a tremendous fire in the square of the city [*in maydano, seu platea civitatis*]. They proposed to burn these four men to prove to the followers of Mohammed (if the four should not be preserved from the flames) that Christians were in error. But if they escaped unharmed, the Christian doctrine ought to be believed as true. The martyrs replied that they would gladly suffer the fire or any other torments for Christ. . . .

The first to be thrown into the flames was Friar James of Padua. Fortified by the sign of the cross, his arms thrown wide and his eyes raised to heaven, he praised God with a pure heart in the midst of the flames — as if he were walking in a pleasant garden of roses and other flowers. James remained unhurt in the raging fire until the fuel was consumed. Not even a hair or a thread of his habit perished.

When the mob saw this phenomenon, they cried out with one mind, "These men are holy; they are men of God. It is a crime to offend them whose way of life is guaranteed by such a marvel."

But the Cadi, seeing the disturbance of the people and fearing lest they should be converted, shouted out: "These men are not holy. This one has escaped from the fire unhurt because he was wearing clothes made of wool from the land of Abraham,[3] whom the Lord has blessed! Send him back naked, and you will see that the way of life he so boasts of will profit him nothing!"

The Cadi ordered James stripped and washed all over so that any protection he might have received from magical incantation would be washed away. Then James was rubbed with oil and butter and placed atop a pyre twice as high as before. Oil and resin were poured over the pyre besides. But He Who saved James the first time willed that the second fire should not harm him — that

---

3. Even followers of Islam revered Jewish tradition and held Palestine a "holy land," since their eclectic religion draws so heavily on the tradition of the Hebrews.

he should not even smell from the flames. His companions thanked God on their knees and praised the fire and the friar who was thrown into its flames.

The mob called out, "This man is a saint. He deserves to be called the servant of God!"

The governor saw the commotion among the people. He heartily embraced Friar James — whose clothes were restored to him — as well as his companions. He told them: "My brothers, I perceive that you *are* servants of God and that your teaching, proven in the fire, is good. I do not will that you suffer any more, nor that anyone else torment you. Go, and leave this land in peace, so that malicious enemies may not lie in wait for your blood. The Cadi wanted to remove you from the land of the living. His followers are treacherous, so leave as rapidly as possible." . . .

The next night [after the friars had departed] the enraged Cadi accused the governor of the worst irreligion, stating that he had betrayed the people and exposed them to countless errors and superstitions. Then the Cadi remarked that he would take up the matter with the governor's superiors. . . . The fearful governor finally assented to the wicked desire of the Cadi and gave him four men to follow the friars and slay them. Then, to demonstrate his observation of the Mohammedan law, the governor had all the Christians of the city put into prison.

The executioners made their way in the middle of the night to capture the martyrs while they were singing matins at the place where they stopped. Friar Peter was not there at the moment of capture. The other three were taken into a field and tied to the trunk of an overhanging tree. The executioners told the Franciscans that they had the order from the governor and the Cadi to kill them. They grieved because the execution was unjust; nevertheless they had to carry out orders.

Fearlessly, serenely, the friars answered: "Beloved friends, do what you have been bidden. It is our hope to win eternal life by the death of our bodies."

A Nestorian Christian who was accompanying the executioners opposed them fiercely and ardently, but to no avail. The habits were dragged from the friars even as they exhorted one another to bear death bravely for Christ. The same Friar James who had been preserved from the fire was killed first; they split open his skull down to his eyes. They killed Friar Thomas of Tolentino second, as he was praying on his knees with folded hands. They wounded him with an arrow, then cut him down by thrusting a sword through his shoulder. He repeated the words "Holy Mary" in a loud voice from where he lay on the earth, until one of the executioners strangled him. The third, Friar Demetrius, they killed by a wound in the breast, a sword through his stomach and many blows until he finally died. The executioners then chopped off the heads of the friars and cut their bodies into pieces.

CHAPTER 10

Continuation of
Wadding's Narrative

When this ruthless crime was done, the dark night was suddenly lighted up with surpassing brightness. The hidden moon shone with unexpected light. It was as bright as midday, and everyone was stupefied. Immediately afterward there was terrifying thunder, lightning, flashes of light, and hail. The like of it had never been seen before in that country. The men standing about [the place of martyrdom] thought that death was upon them. . . .

Nevertheless, the executioners did not repent even in the face of such wonders and heavenly signs. In fact, they returned to the house where the friars had been staying to plunder whatever might have been left there by them. There they came upon Friar Peter at prayer; he did not know what had happened to his confriars.

The executioners led Friar Peter, bound, to the Cadi. Despite the offer of a great reward, he could not move the friar to renounce the Christian faith. Peter just repeated the praise of Christ and the damnation of Mohammed. The friar was ordered to be led to prison, and to be taken forth the next day for a special questioning on the faith.

Peter replied with constancy to every question. They tortured him from morning till evening. But neither blows nor scourging could induce him to pronounce the Mohammedan profession of faith, *Allah Il Allah,* even with his lips. Nor could they extract from him a denial of the Catholic profession of the mystery of the Trinity.

At the end, beaten almost to death, the friar was hanged by a noose from a tree. He hung there for two whole days without dying or even showing signs of weakness. He glorified God and urged those who came near him to accept the faith of Christ, until the governor heard of it. He ordered the Franciscan taken down and led to a field to be decapitated. Friar Peter's martyrdom was on Saturday before Palm Sunday, just before the sun set [*sub hora vesperarum*].

The next day some Nestorians came from their hiding places to take away the body. They were unable to locate the remains: there was not even a trace of blood where the friar had been slain. As they stood in amazement, not knowing what to say, a certain pious man came up to them. He told the Nestorians that it was revealed to him that the venerable body of the holy martyr had been carried away by angels and buried with the blood that had been spilled; that in due time it would be uncovered.

At the same time all four Franciscan martyrs appeared to a Christian of the city. Because of their shining radiance, the Christian asked them if they were still alive. They replied that their life was one of glory and heavenly delights, without a care. The Christian then asked the martyrs another question: What had happened to their companion, Friar Jordanus.[1] They replied that Jordanus' boat had already docked in port.

Because the people feared the Cadi, the bodies of the first three martyrs lay for fourteen days in the field where they had been killed. When Friar Jordanus discovered them, he found the relics exuding not a nauseating but a sweet odor; the bodies were soft and fresh, and appeared as if they had just been slain on that day. With the help of a young man of Genoa, the Dominican collected their remains. . . .

The Lord did not will that the murder of His servants should go unpunished. He began to exact justice from the governor's friend, the judge who agreed to the Cadi's will in every request. As he rode through the city on the day after the martyrdom, he fell from his horse. He died as he struck the ground.

The governor himself, moved by avarice, demanded that the possessions of the martyrs[2] be delivered to him.

---

1. This is the same Dominican, Friar Jordanus, who has been mentioned before. He had been traveling with the four Franciscans and had even reached Tana with them — which explains the question of the Christian to whom the four appeared. Jordanus had gone on to another mission for the time being, but was miraculously guided to return in order to recover the relics of his four companions. Friar Jordanus himself appears indelibly as a heroic character and an inspiring representative of his Order in the East.

2. It is difficult to see what valuables such poor friars could have had with them. Perhaps they were taking gifts from the Pope or a European ruler to the khans of Tartary.

When he could not extort these, because the executioners had already plundered them after the murder, the governor threw two Christians, friends of the martyrs, into prison. As the governor lay sleeping on the following night, these four glorious martyrs appeared at the four corners of his bed, brandishing flaming swords and threatening death if he would not deal humanely with Christians.

The governor began to shout and call for the aid of his servants, to whom he told the vision, describing how the innocent men whom he had killed were threatening him with death. Early the next morning he hurried to the Cadi to tell him the story. He asked the Cadi how to avert the wrath of the friars and the punishment of God.

"By almsgiving and by honoring their memory," responded the Cadi.

There and then the governor ordered the Christians released from their chains and humbly begged their pardon. He ordered by a public proclamation that no one, under pain of death, dare injure anyone professing the Christian doctrine. He permitted all Christians who had fled the city under pressure of mobs and persecution to return freely and live among the Moslems without the least fear.

Next the governor prepared a sumptuous banquet for the poor and gave large alms to the needy. He ordered four little mosques [*mesquitas parvas*], or oratories, to be built in memory of the martyrs.

By the power of the right hand of the Most High many men were converted to the faith and were baptized by Friar Jordanus. The Cadi threatened death to all who

deserted the Mohammedan law, and began to scheme for a
new persecution against Christians.

The Lord, however, was not moved by the reparation
of the governor after the unjust and cruel death of the
martyrs. The Lord caused the sultan [his superior] to
turn against the governor for the wicked sentence enacted
against men whose innocence and virtue God had demon-
strated by so many miracles. So the sultan ordered the
governor and his whole family to suffer the exact penalty
given to the four Franciscans, for the crime of the governor was that he despised the wonders worked by God
and condemned to death men whose virtue was guaranteed
by amazing signs. The Cadi, realizing what punishment
was being prepared for him, immediately fled from the
territory.

Blessed Friar Odoric of Friuli, of the Province of
St. Anthony, while he was sowing the word of God in
some of the cities of India, heard of the heroic passion of
the four martyrs. He reached Tana, as he himself tells
us, to learn the entire story and to carry the holy remains
away with him. . . .

CHAPTER 11

Along the West Coast of India

"Afterward I, Friar Odoric, knowing of their glorious martyrdom, went there [Tana]. And I took their remains from the sepulcher to which they had been committed." Thus the friar begins his travelogue anew. But he is far from done with the marvels of his heroic confriars. He wrapped his treasures in towels [*toaleis*] to prepare their transit to China. It was to be a long voyage: around the pepper-growing coast of India, across the sea to the East Indian Islands, and finally over to China.

But we are getting ahead of our story. Leaving Tana, Friar Odoric was to sail down the coast to a city called Polumbum. The place has been identified variously with Colombo on the Island of Ceylon, with Kail to the east of Cape Comorin — southernmost point of the whole peninsula — and with Quilon to the west of the Cape.[1]

---

1. Cf. Yule-Cordier, *op. cit.*, Vol. II, pp. 129-130, footnote 1.

The story loses nothing when related in Odoric's own words:

"I was voyaging by sea with these bones to a city called Polumbum, where pepper grows in abundance. The wind slacked off completely. The idolaters aboard began to petition their gods to grant them a favorable breeze — which their gods, of course, were utterly unable to accomplish.

"Next the Saracens [Mohammedans] exhausted themselves in praying for a wind. Naturally, they effected nothing by their supplications either.

"Finally they ordered my companion and me to beseech our God to grant us the wind. Had we been successful, the men aboard would have paid us great veneration. The captain of the ship added in the Armenian language, so that the others could not understand, 'But if we don't get the wind, overboard with those bones of yours.'

"With the captain's words in our ears, my companion and I prayed to God for wind. When we saw the wind was still not forthcoming, we promised many Masses in honor of the glorious Virgin, just so we might have a little wind. But not even then did we have any success.

"As a final resort, I took one of the bones of the martyrs and gave it to our servant. I instructed him to hurry to the bow [*caput*] of the ship and quickly throw the relic into the sea.

"As soon as the bone was cast into the sea, a favorable wind began to blow. It did not slack off until we reached port. It was only by the merits of these martyred brethren of ours that we arrived in safety."

This is the simple tale Odoric dictated as he lay sick in Padua. He must have thanked God once again for the intercession of the four martyrs granted to him a dozen years earlier in distant India, among hostile idolaters and Moslems. God withheld His succor and the Virgin her aid, for it was the divine will to draw attention to the holiness of the murdered Franciscans.

The city of Polumbum and the coastal region north of it are more fully spoken of by the friar than any other place at which he stopped before. The coastal region was known as Malabar. Odoric spells it *Minibar* or *Mimbar*. The pepper groves were so extensive that Malabar was synonymous with its main product. Odoric claims that an eighteen days' journey was necessary to traverse the length of the pepper grove he himself saw. The natives trained the vines to grow on tall trees. The peppers were gathered in bunches, like grapes, when still green. When the sun dried the pepper, it was stored away in containers.

The citizens of Polumbum did not impress Odoric very favorably, although the place was a merchandise mart of the first rank. The friar does not cavil at the fact the people of Polumbum wore only a loincloth; he merely mentions it. But how he must have felt about their worship of the bovine species — worship which he calls abominable — is evident from the following description:

"All the natives of the region worship cattle as divine. They claim the cattle are sacred beasts. For six years the natives put them to work, but during the seventh year, they are allowed to roam freely in public [*bos ... positus est in communi:* the village commune, or the public square].

"The people have an abominable ritual which they observe in the following way. Every morning they bring two basins [*bacilia*] of gold or silver to the stables. The natives place these basins under the cattle when they are led from the stable. In one of these basins they catch the urine of the cattle, in the other basin the dung.

"They bathe their faces in the urine. Next they smear on their own foreheads, on both cheekbones, and in the middle of their chest, the dung they have saved. In four places, therefore, do the natives place the excrement of the cattle. When they have done with this ceremony, they say they are sanctified for the whole day. This is done not only by the common people, but even by the king and queen."

This ridiculous and degrading ritual brings home to us how perverted religious observance can become without the divinely guided Church. Nor was the idolatrous worship of cattle limited to the ceremony described above. The natives of Polumbum paid divine honors to a god fashioned in the likeness half of a man and half of an ox. This image often spoke out and demanded the blood of fifty virgins. It is peculiar that Odoric does not add whether he thought the words of the idol were somehow diabolical, or the fraud of the pagan priesthood. In any case, parents frequently offered the blood of their sons and daughters to the idol. As one manuscript of Odoric's travelogue concludes, this practice in India was as ordinary as the European custom of devoting one's children to monastic life before the children reached their majority.

Odoric disdains to tell us any more of the customs of these people save one. This is the practice of the suttee, which the British Government in India did so much to eradicate during the nineteenth century.

When a man died, his relatives cremated his living wife along with the corpse. It was only right, they believed, that the wife should accompany her husband into the next world. A woman could avoid the suttee, however, if she had borne sons to her husband and chose to remain with them. In this matter, as in so many others, men were more privileged: a man could take another woman to wife when his first one died.

Odoric closes his whole narrative of the pepper-growing country of Polumbum with the comment, "It is far better not to mention the many other amazing and bestial things which happen there."

It must have been frustrating to the friar to witness the disgusting observances practiced by these people and not be able to stay among them and preach Christ to them. But his mission was to Cathay, and in that direction he had to hasten.

CHAPTER 12

Ceylon and Dondin

 Friar Odoric wrote that he traveled on a *junk* from Polumbum to China. This was probably the traditional Chinese sailing vessel still common in that country, where mechanized travel has not replaced the junk and the sampan. The various manuscripts spell the word in Latin as *zuncum, conchum* and *lonclum*. By these names or any other, the boat remains a junk.

Our friar was in luck if that was the kind of vessel he was sailing in, since it meant that it was shipping out for China, his own destination, even though it would be many months before he arrived there. The boat carried him to Ceylon, the islands of Dondin, Java, Sumatra, and perhaps to Borneo and the Spice Islands. The location of these stopping places is not made too clear — as is to be expected in the absence of maps to which Odoric might direct his reader. Before he went the rounds of these many islands, however, he sailed around the southern tip of India, Cape Comorin, stopped at Ceylon and visited the eastern coast of the peninsula. Since Odoric dictated the story of his visit to Dondin immediately after describing Ceylon, let us follow that itinerary, even though we are uncertain as to Dondin's location.

Though Odoric visited Ceylon, he cannot have circumnavigated it completely: he tells us that the island is two thousand miles in circumference! Undoubtedly he merely disembarked at Ceylon as the ship passed between it and the mainland.

Ceylon was celebrated for two reasons: its gems and the Mountain of Adam. Other contemporaries of Odoric also mention the local legend of Adam's Mountain.

The story goes that Father Adam sat on this mountain in the interior of the island — how he got there is not a part of the story — and for a full hundred years wept for his wicked son Cain. Close by was the lake that was formed from the outpouring of his tears. Strangely enough for a medieval, Odoric discounts the story as a mere legend, for he himself says he saw that the lake was fed by underground streams or springs. It is a pity that Odoric did not exhibit similar reservation of opinion about the things told him elsewhere — especially of those places he did not have the opportunity to visit. And yet, it is to the friar's credit that very little of what he wrote cannot be verified by modern scholarship.

Now at the bottom of the lake of "Adam's tears" precious stones were found in abundance, especially rubies. Perhaps they were washed down by mountain streams and rain, or deposited by natural forces underground, such as the erosion caused by water. The difficulty in recovering the gems was due to the reeds and bloodsuckers[1] which infested the water and made it perilous for a diver to search the bottom for the precious stones.

The local ruler was in no need of the gems for himself. The wealth of the island and its commercially strategic location at the very middle point of the sea lane around the Indian peninsula assured him of lucrative business. But the ruler permitted his poorer subjects to retrieve the gems once or twice each year. In order to protect themselves from the hungry leeches among the growth at the bottom of the lake, the natives rubbed themselves all over with lemon juice, for the citric acid repelled the parasites.

Taking leave of Ceylon and the Mountain of Adam, Odoric sailed on the Chinese junk to the Island of Dondin. Where Dondin actually lies is a problem for linguists and geographers to solve. As always, the lesson Odoric himself learns and strives to teach his readers concerns the native religious customs and moral ignorance. Let us follow his eyewitness description of the island and its people:

"I disembarked at an island called Dondin — which means the same as *Unclean.* Wicked men inhabit the island. They eat raw flesh and just about every other repulsive thing one can name.

"They observe a custom that is especially vile. A father will eat his own son, and a son his father. A wife

---

1. The text here can be read either as *yrundinibus et sanguisugis* or (*h*)*irudinibus et sanguisugis.* The first is *reeds and bloodsuckers,* the second is *leeches and bloodsuckers.* The confusion may be due to some copyist's mistake.

will eat her own husband, and the husband his wife. This rite is observed in the following way.

"Suppose someone's father is ailing. His son will ask the advice of an astrologer and of a priest: 'Sir, inquire of our god whether my father will be freed of his sickness or must die of it.'

"Both the priest and the sick man's son approach their idol — which is made of gold or silver — and pray. 'Lord, you are our god. We adore you as divine. Reply to what we are about to ask you. A man is sick with a certain infirmity. We beg you to answer whether he will die or be freed of this sickness.'

"Then a demon answers by the mouth of the image. 'Your father will not die, but will be freed from his sickness. Take this precaution and he will get well.' Then the evil spirit explains the manner in which the son must care for his father. When he returns home to his father, the son takes diligent care of him, till the father is relieved of his condition.

"But if the evil spirit says the father is to die, the priest comes to the home and smothers his face so that the man will suffocate and die where he lies. They cut the dead man into small pieces. Then they invite their friends, relatives [*parentes*] and all the entertainers of the whole district [*hystriones*]. The corpse is eaten with singing and great display of merriment. The bones of the dead person they collect to be interred with much solemnity. Any relative who is absent from the merry-making [*nuptias*] considers it disgraceful not to have been present.

"I remonstrated with some of them," continues Odoric. " 'Why do you carry on so, if what you do is obviously against natural reason? If one dog is killed and set before another, even the dog would not touch the carcass. Neither should you who are supposed to be reasonable human beings.'

"They replied: 'The only reason why we keep this custom is to prevent the worms from consuming the dead man's body. If worms were allowed to feed on the corpse, his soul would suffer terrible pain. We eat his flesh to prevent his soul from suffering.'

"I could talk to them for as long as I wanted, but they simply did not choose to believe me, nor to discontinue this custom."

The most curious part of Odoric's story here is not the custom — barbaric to us though it seems — of suffocating the hopelessly sick and eating their remains. In fact, many other primitive peoples demonstrate filial piety in stranger ways. Among Eskimos, for instance, it is sometimes considered a "merciful" way of disposing of the aged to leave old people to freeze to death in an abandoned igloo; and certain Indian tribes leave helpless or feeble members of the tribe alone in the wilderness during a tribal migration. This is not so much malice as a misdirected evidence of filial devotion, based on the presumption that these unfortunates would not wish to burden the tribe any longer.

No, the curious part of Odoric's narrative is the talking idol, which gave the instructions to the priests and relatives of the ailing people. Did the friar simply accept the voice of the idol as that of a demon? Evidently he did, since the replies are not attributed to any human machination.

An idol spoken through by an evil spirit is not to be shrugged off. Wherever the influence of Christ is less manifest, the "prince of this world" holds court. Besides — and here is the most cogent argument — primitive people who live on close terms with danger and who are not strangers to poverty, sickness and violence, are often fatalistic. The people of Dondin were quite apt to have worshiped a principle of evil, just as true worshipers pay divine honors to the principle of good, which is God. Of course these natives would not be worshiping the devil as the opponent of Christ. Rather, they would be trying to propitiate that wicked force in the world, which to them, at least, appeared more powerful than the good. This is no uncommon religious phenomenon among less civilized peoples.

With the story of the natives of Dondin who kill their sick and devour the bodies, Odoric feels that he has said enough incredible things about the place. His closing words indicate that he does not expect people to believe everything he has written, though by no means has he exhausted his tales:

"Many other wonders of this place I do not mention. Unless a man sees them, he can scarcely believe them. There are not so many wonders in all the world as one can find in India alone. I have dictated only the things which I was able to certify and which are without doubt as I have narrated."

CHAPTER 13

Mobar

After rounding Cape Comorin and visiting Ceylon, Odoric sailed northward along the eastern coast of the Indian peninsula into the region he calls Mobar. It is not to be confused with Malabar, lying on the west coast of the peninsula almost exactly opposite.

Of the points of interest he thinks his readers will be most pleased to hear about, the tomb of St. Thomas the Apostle is first. Unfortunate to record, pagan idolaters made the shrine of the saint just another temple of their worship; they adorned what was originally a Christian oratory with scores of false idols. We must remember, however, that India was out of contact with Catholicism and Rome for a thousand years before thirteenth-century accounts and notices began to trickle through again. The heretical and sometimes debased Nestorian Christian sect would have exerted little or no effort to eradicate idolatrous superstition creeping into doctrine and practice. The Nestorians were the only "representatives" of Christianity in India and China for that thousand-year period.

The most adequate description of the tomb of St. Thomas is found in Odoric's direct and simple story of the idolatrous people who lived along the coastal region of Mobar, where the Apostle was buried:

"In the kingdom of Mobar the body of blessed Thomas the Apostle is buried. But the church in which he lies is filled with countless idols. Close by there are about fifteen houses, which belong to Nestorians and some other Christians who are wicked heretics.

"An amazing idol is likewise found here. People from all over India come to venerate it. The image is as tall as St. Christopher is ordinarily portrayed by painters. It is made of solid gold and stands on a huge pedestal [*cathedram*], which is also of gold. They have placed a string of precious jewels — a necklace of great value — around the neck of the image.

"The shrine of this idol is constructed of pure gold. The entire roof is of gold, as well as the floor.

"Just as Christians come from afar to St. Peter's [in Rome], the natives travel great distances to pray before this idol. Some of them make their way to the shrine with a rope bound to their neck as a penance. Others come with their hands tied to a board across their shoulders [*super unam tabulam ad collum ligatum*]. Others make a pilgrimage with a dagger [*cultello*] driven into an arm. They do not remove the dagger until they reach the idol, and as a result, by this time their arm is entirely putrefied [*marcidum*].

"Some of the natives devise other kinds of asceticism. For example, a man might take three steps at a time from the moment he left his home far away. At the fourth step he would make a reverence prone on the ground his full length [*faciunt unam veniam ita longam super terram sicut unus illorum esset*]. Finally he might go so far as to use a thurible and incense the whole length of his prostration [*etiam igne adolentes desuper illam longitudinem veniae ipsius*].

"With such a demonstration of his piety a person might travel the whole journey to the idol, even if it were to take a very long time to reach it, without failing to observe this ceremony. If the person should wish to delay his progress for some reason, he would make a sign to indicate how far he had come. And this is the procedure till the idol itself is approached.

"At the shrine of this idol there is an artificial lake. When the pilgrims reach it, they throw gold, silver, or precious stones into the lake. Their idea is to do honor to the idol and help keep the shrine in repair. Wherefore there is an immense treasure in the lake of gold, silver and jewels. When the caretakers need anything for the shrine, they search the bottom of the lake for whatever has been cast into it.

"On the day which is sacred to the idol, the people congregate from all around. They take the idol from the shrine and carry it on a magnificent chariot [*curru*]. The king and queen, every pilgrim arrival, and all the people, with whoever else may be present, lead the idol forth from the shrine with loud chanting and every kind of music they know.

"When the god is out of its temple, many pairs of
maidens walk before it singing a wondrous melody.
Behind the maidens walk the pilgrims, who have come
especially for this festival; and they throw themselves
under the wheels of the chariot so that it cuts across their
bodies. Thus do they wish to die for their god. As the
chariot passes over them, it breaks their bones and even
cuts their bodies in two. They die on the spot.[1]

"This then is the manner in which the procession
moves to some designated place, from which they lead the
idol back to its original pedestal with songs and musical
instruments as before. A year does not pass but more than
five hundred men die by suicide in this way. The natives
take the corpses and burn them. They say their remains
are holy because these pilgrims vowed to sacrifice themselves to the god.

"These people have even another means of self-sacri-
fice. A man will say, 'I am resolved to commit suicide
for my god.' His parents, friends and all the entertainers
of the district gather to make merry. They hang five sharp
daggers about his neck and lead him before the idol. The
suicide takes a very sharp blade into his hand and cries out
in a loud voice, 'For my god I cut away a piece of flesh
from my own body!'

---

1. This is one of the first references to a Middle Eastern religious
ceremony that has become famous by the name of *Juggernaut,* which
is also the name of the chariot or huge cart. Either the wheels of the
vehicle were so broad and the cart itself so heavy that the fanatical
suicides were crushed to death, or the wheels were so narrow and sharp
that they actually cut the bodies in two. Ordinarily, at a ceremony like
the one Odoric describes, some worshipers pulled the huge cart — it
needed many backs to accomplish the pilgrimage — and others piled the
bodies of the suicides upon it, making it heavier with each ghastly burden.

"When the fanatic has actually cut away a piece of flesh from some member of his body, he throws it into the face of the image and says, 'I vow my death to my god.' With these words the man commits suicide then and there for the honor of his god. His corpse is burned at once; it is even considered sacred because he died by his own hand for his god.

"There are besides these stories," Odoric concludes, "many fabulous and amazing rites observed by the natives. But they are better left unwritten."

CHAPTER 14

Through the East Indies

Only a few more stops, a few more months, and Odoric would walk on the soil of China, which was territory immediately subject to the Great Khan of Cathay. After leaving India, Ceylon and Dondin, there was only the southeasterly voyage through the East Indies, then up along the coast of Indo-China. In Odoric's day, of course, East Indies and Indo-China were not the names of these places. However, the names of Sumatra and Java — two places the friar describes in some detail — appear in Odoric's chronicle.

As the map indicates, the Island of Sumatra was the first major island to which the Chinese junk (on which we may presume he was still traveling) carried Odoric and his precious relics. Sumatra is almost exactly bisected by the equator. The heat was so unbearable that no one, relates Odoric, save women with child, wore the least shred of clothing. Such a primitive condition is still not uncommon among some tribes of the East Indies, especially deep in the interior of the larger islands. Among the aborigines of Australia the same custom obtains.

Odoric evidently chided the natives for their lack of modesty. They replied that it was more fitting to go naked. After all, they reasoned, such was Father Adam's own condition when he came from the hand of God. We can scarcely believe that these natives were Christians. Perhaps the reference to Adam is based on some native legend consonant with the account of Genesis. The story of creation is the common heritage of all peoples. Among the primitives, where history and legend are blended into poetry for the sake of being more easily memorized, even after centuries the tradition could have been passed down intact.

In any case, to the islanders, at least, Odoric's habit must have appeared rather senseless garb in the torrid climate along the equator.

The primitive status of some of the natives is even more apparent from the friar's further description. They observed an uncompromising community to a shocking degree. Except for individual houses, they held all things common. This included property, wives and husbands. As Odoric wrote, "When a woman has borne a son or daughter, she gives it to whichever husband she chooses and with whom she has lain; him the woman calls the father of her child."

The final witness of the barbarity of the natives of northern Sumatra was their cannibalism. They ate human flesh as casually as the people of medieval Italy ate animal flesh, Odoric asserts. The natural resources of the island were valuable and much in demand by traders. The natives exchanged their gold, aloes and camphor for live children. These unfortunate victims were sold at the island by unscrupulous traders; the natives later slaughtered the children and ate them. The vivid description of our friar seems to indicate that, if he did not see any such cannibalistic banquet, he may at least have seen the unfortunate victims at the island, since he stopped there. The unfortunate children could scarcely escape from the island; their tender age would of itself disable them from devising means of fleeing. And if they did escape, it would only be to perish in the sea or in some interior jungle.

Unable to evangelize the natives and convert them to the gentler ways of Christianity, how Odoric's heart must have been torn at the knowledge of such abominations! It appears that his main reason for narrating the barbaric customs and debased religious rites, to the exclusion of other characteristics of the peoples he saw in the Orient, was to awaken in his brethren back home the desire to give themselves to missionary work among the uncivilized.

In southern Sumatra the conditions were no better. Here the men and women were wont to tattoo themselves with hot irons in a dozen places on their face [*generatio gentis singularis signantis se ferro calido parvo bene in duodecim locis in facie*].

In Java, Friar Odoric visited the palace of the king. We do not know where the royal city was located, but we are certain that the king was a powerful monarch. He had seven other kings subject to his sovereignty and the allegiance of a well-populated island [*multum bene populatur*].

The income from the spice traffic and the tribute from his seven royal subjects could not have been small, for the splendor of his house is worthy of a tale from *The Arabian Nights*. In fact, not even the khans of Cathay were able to subjugate the king of Java or vindicate their demands for tribute, because the king was so far away and so powerful in his own right.

The palace was the chief source of wonder to Odoric [*valde mirabile*]. The structure itself was huge. Its staircases were broad and high, and the stairs were alternately of gold and silver. Even the floor was made with alternate bricks of gold and silver. The walls were laminated on the interior with plates of gold evidently made to form a continuous frieze, for the friar wrote that horsemen were sculptured on the walls out of the pure gold. In the same way Christian artists represent the saints, the Javanese sculptor added halos set with jewels about the heads of the horsemen. Finally, even the roof was made of gold, or more probably plated with the precious metal. Odoric does not hesitate to call the palace of the Javanese king richer and more beautiful than any in the whole world. And this is the opinion of a man who spent three years at the imperial court of Cathay.

It is not hard to imagine the effect of such wealth on Odoric. His idea of what comprised a huge fortune and what constituted large-scale trading — even measured by the cities of Venice and Genoa that he knew so well — must have changed completely. The trade and the flow of money from Asia Minor, Mesopotamia, Persia, and India would have staggered any imagination. Odoric was accustomed to seeing gold and jewels on sacred vessels, vestments and altar appurtenances, and on the trappings of noble persons; but in the Orient he found sizable idols, temples and palaces whose very building materials were the precious metals.

We will never know how Odoric conducted himself in the presence of the Javanese king and his court. Did he preach there too? Did he try to reason them out of their debased customs, as he tried elsewhere? Did he baptize? Did he have to use an interpreter? Did he, for instance, have to prostrate himself before the king, if that was court procedure?

So little is known of the islands at which the friar stopped, so little of the people and their civilization, that Odoric's travelogue merely highlights what he remembered after fourteen years of moving all over the Orient; the rest is merely conjecture. As it is, we can only guess that some kind merchant agreed to carry Odoric to China, but only by way of the islands at which the boat itself had to touch. Of this we can be sure, however: Odoric's heart ached for the simple but misguided natives; his limbs were untiring during his investigation; his face was always turned toward Cathay.

It is not certain, but it appears probable, that Odoric went on to Borneo. It is as likely a guess that he stopped at the island of Celebes and the Spice Islands. At any rate, the friar says the sea which lay behind the whole archipelago was called the Dead Sea [*Mare Mortuum*]. A strong current carried off any foolhardy sailors who chanced even a short voyage offshore. Perhaps Odoric believed that the water running south fell off the edge of the earth [*aqua cuius semper currit versus meridiem*]!

Odoric refers to the inhabitants of this last island, which may have been Borneo, as users of poisoned arrows and blowguns. The tips of the arrows were dipped into a vegetable poison and inserted into the end of a hollow cane, probably of bamboo. When the enemy was sighted, the hidden assailant blew swiftly and sharply into the cane to propel the light arrow. This silent death was an excellent means of ambushing even a large group of the enemy. The blowgun was the ordinary weapon for battle and for hunting wild animals. Some of the poisons used by the natives did not contaminate the whole animal and the carcass could be used for food.

Our friar describes how sago was made in those islands of the East Indies. Whether Italians of Odoric's day ate as much spaghetti as they do nowadays is a separate question; but Odoric offers some comment on the sago. "It makes the tastiest starch food in the whole world [*pastam bonam de mundo*]. From the paste they can make whatever they choose, either ordinary starch foods or excellent bread, of which I, Friar Odoric, have eaten. I have seen all these things with my own eyes."

I wonder if Odoric himself believed the next story he told of the islanders. He appears to report it as fact, but he may only have heard of it.

The natives found a strange use for a creeping plant, which took root from its own low-lying foliage, much like crab grass. Odoric calls it *casan*. In the elbows of this grass the plant formed a stony substance of some kind [*lapides*]. The belief of the natives was that if one wore a bit of the hard secretion on his person, he could not be injured by iron weapons of any kind. It was the common practice of the men of the tribe to wear a chip of the rocky substance at all times. When the boys were still quite young, the older men would gash them in their arms and press a bit of the plant secretion into the wound, so that the gash healed around it. It was even possible to close the wound immediately by using a powder made from some kind of fish [*pulvere unius piscis*].

So invulnerable did the islanders consider themselves in regard to wounds made by iron weapons, that they dared to engage in profitable piracy. And the merchants they attacked were similarly impressed by the current superstition, for Odoric says that they had to make their defensive weapons of hard wood instead.

This is the last of Odoric's tales of the East Indies.

CHAPTER 15

China at Last

After months of sailing among the East Indian islands, Friar Odoric set foot on the mainland once again. But it was just to touch on the shore of Cochin China, probably for water and supplies. At that time, Cochin China was called Zampa. Despite his short stay there, Odoric found cause for much wonderment in the multiplicity of the king's elephants and wives. Plurality in either case — of elephants or of wives — could not have astounded Odoric any more by this time; but the king of Zampa received a commemoration in Odoric's chronicle by the amazing achievement of producing over two hundred offspring.

Odoric thought that Cochin China was just another island in the East Indian Archipelago, stretching from Ceylon to the coast of China proper. It is easy to understand how he made this mistake: two gulfs lie, one northeast and one southwest, of Cochin China.

Zampa was the last stop, and Odoric found himself in China at last, and within the jurisdiction of the Great Khan, the fabulous potentate to whom the Church had sent this Franciscan missionary. To Odoric, China was "Upper India." He named it thus probably because it lies north of India — and we may assume that the friar considered the East Indies a single geographical entity with India itself.

The Province of Manzi was Odoric's first stop in China. Manzi boasted over two thousand cities, Odoric claims, which were larger than the cities of Treviso or Vicenza in Italy. The Chinese population even then was innumerable, but two thousand cities is an evident exaggeration. Nevertheless, Odoric's claim is undoubtedly true that in some parts of the Province of Manzi there were more people than one saw in Venice on Ascension Thursday — which was the gala festival day of the espousal of the city with the Adriatic Sea, into which the ruling doge of Venice threw a ring, and the day on which the Venetian fair began.

The port of Odoric's disembarkation was Canton, written by him as Cens-Kalan. It was there that the Chinese face caught his attention and fancy.

"The men," wrote the friar, "are rather handsome [*corpore pulchri*], but pale. Their beards are sparse and long, like a cat's whiskers [murilegae, id est cattae]. But the women are really the loveliest in the whole world."

The city of Canton was three times as large as Venice. Odoric gauged all the larger cities on his itinerary by his memory of Venice, which many of his readers would have had occasion to see. And yet Venice is always

smaller by comparison. The reason for Canton's pros-
perity as a trading post along the sea lanes of the China
Sea was its huge natural harbor. Besides, of the larger
cities of coastal China, Canton lay closest to the Indies
and to India itself.

It was said in a foregoing chapter that Odoric's story
about the bones of the Tana martyrs had not all been told.
The purpose was to include it here because the final wonder he relates about these precious relics concerns his
passage to Canton.

"The idolaters [of the city of Canton] have this
custom," says the friar. "Before a vessel is moored, they
come to look the whole ship over to learn what is aboard.
Now if they find the remains of dead persons on the
vessel, the customs officers throw the remains overboard
at once; they believe death hangs close over the pos-
sessor's head.

"Although they searched the boat according to their
wont, the officers discovered nothing at all, despite the
large size of the martyrs' relics. Under such protection of
God we carefully brought the relics to the house of our
brethren [in Zayton], where they are appropriately en-
tombed with honor and great reverence."

Many are the remarks which Odoric inserts into his
chronicle about the peculiarities of the Province of Manzi.
There are two that bear repetition, because people of the
West still associate these customs with China.

The first custom belonged to the men of Manzi, and
only to the wellborn. Their fingernails were a source of
constant care to them: they guarded them to prevent
the nails from breaking, and let them grow to an enormous

length. It was the sign of noble breeding. Odoric mentions that some of the men's thumbnails grew in a curve around the tip of the thumb into the palm of the hand [*cum ipsis circumdant sibi manus*]. Perhaps this custom indicated that the bearers of long fingernails were men of leisure, since laborers could hardly keep such a growth very long.

The second custom belonged to the women of Manzi. They considered it an indispensable adjunct to their beauty to have small feet. Therefore, as most of us already know, the mothers bound the feet of their daughters directly from infancy. The tightly bandaged feet were characteristic of only wellborn women at that time, just as long nails represented the breeding of the noblemen. The bound feet were probably the result of a similar notion that such painfully crippled feet, dainty though they were supposed to look, could not belong to working women. Both customs still prevail in some parts of China, especially where the practicality of the West has not robbed China of all her centuries-long traditions.

Odoric mentions several important cities throughout Manzi. Among them was the city of Zayton, to which Odoric was carrying the relics from Tana. It too rivaled Erzerum, Ormuz, and Canton as a center of commerce. Best of all, Odoric found here the relief of living under a Franciscan roof once again — the first time since he had left the city of Soltania in Persia, thousands of land and sea miles away. He tells us that the friars already had two houses in Zayton, which indicates the extent of their evangelization in this foreign country. We open the

subsequent chapter with a short description of the establishment of the Order in Zayton, as recorded by its Franciscan bishop, Andrew of Perugia, in a letter written in
1326, or only a few years after Odoric stayed there.

CHAPTER 16

Zayton

"Friar Andrew of Perugia of the Order of Friars Minor, by divine permission called to be Bishop, sends health and eternal peace in the Lord to the Reverend Friar Guardian of our friary at Perugia.

"Because of the tremendous distance over land and sea between us, I can scarcely hope that my letter will reach your hands. . . .

"You remember that I and my confriar Peregrin, the sole companion of my travels, by the help of God finally reached Cambalec. We have undergone many labors and fatigue, hunger, and various sufferings both by land and by sea. In fact, once we were even despoiled of our habits.

"Cambalec is the capital of the Great Khan's empire, at which we arrived in 1317, as I recall. According to the Apostolic See, we consecrated the archbishop [John of Monte Corvino], with whom we remained about five years. During this period we

85

received an *alafa* from the generous emperor for the food
and clothing of eight persons. An *alafa* is a pension which
the emperor gives to messengers of powerful men, to
public speakers, warriors, various kinds of craftsmen,
entertainers, poor people, and others. The total of the
pensions surpasses the expenditures of many European
kings. . . .

"There is an important city on the seacoast, which is
called Zayton in the Persian tongue. A wealthy Armenian
lady has built a large and beautiful church for us there,
and endowed it with a large enough benefice. It was
given the rank of cathedral by the archbishop [in
Cambalec] at her request. The Armenian lady gave the
church to our Friar-Bishop Gerard, and to the other friars
with him; she willed the place permanently to us at her
death.

"Friar Gerard was the first bishop. When he died
in Zayton, where we likewise buried him, the archbishop
wanted to make me his successor. At my refusal he
bestowed the episcopate on Peregrin, whom I have mentioned at the beginning of my letter. Peregrin governed
the diocese for a few years and died in 1322. . . .

"I was able to persuade the emperor to transfer the
alafa, or pension, to Zayton, which is a three weeks'
journey from Cambalec. . . . In a grove about a quarter of
a mile from Zayton, I built another church, fitted to our
needs and quite lovely. It has a friary attached with
accommodations for twelve friars and four rooms good
enough to house any prelate.

"A short while after the demise of Friar Peregrin,
I received a rescript from the archbishop about my being

placed in charge of the cathedral church, to which appointment I agreed. So now I live either there or in the hermitage (on the outskirts of town, as I described above), according to my own discretion.

"I am well in body. As long as life holds out, I can labor for a few more years in this vineyard, although I am already gray from natural infirmity and old age.

"In this vast empire there are people of all nations and sects under heaven. Everyone is allowed to live according to his religious convictions. They believe — or rather, are mistaken in believing — that everyone can be saved by any religion. We are allowed to preach freely and in safety. None of the Jews or Saracens is ever converted. But a very large number [*quam plurimi*] of idolaters have been baptized. Many of these latter, however, do not continue on the way of Christianity. . . .

"Given at Zayton in January in the year of our Lord 1326."[1]

This letter from the Friar-Bishop Andrew about the history of his own diocese in the Chinese Province of Manzi gives us at least a sketch of the missions there as Odoric passed through and left the relics of the Tana martyrs. His arrival was the occasion of much excitement, no doubt, for he was bringing the latest news from back home. These friars were quartered in a foreign city, surrounded by hostile religionists, far from relative, friend or even confriar. Odoric could have told them how the brethren fared in Persia, where last he stayed in a friary of the Order. The news of Italy, and of the papacy — then removed to Avignon — would be on his lips, and

---

1. L. Wadding, *Annales Minorum*, Vol. VII, pp. 53 sq.

he would be able to report on the emperor and kings and princes of the West.

The friars in Zayton, on the other hand, would have briefed Odoric on how to behave among the Cathayans, since they all had been to court. They would have told him of the procedure to be followed in the presence of the Great Khan, on whom so much of their success and support depended — at least from a material point of view. Finally, they would have sent a written and verbal report with Odoric to their Ordinary — or religious superior — in Cambalec, John of Monte Corvino.

Armed with precautions and reports, Odoric continued northward by land toward the imperial court. He took notice of the two methods of fishing he had not seen before either at home or in his travels throughout the East. His story gains by being told in his own words, and so we have translated the passage from his chronicle. At the time, the friar was passing the coastal area cut through and watered by the many branches of the Yangtze River.

"I stopped at a city," he writes, "which has a bridge across the river. I stayed as a guest in a home which stood at one extremity of the bridge. While I was there, my host desired to provide some enjoyable pastime.

" 'If you want to see some clever fishing,' he said, 'come along with me.'

"He led me onto the bridge. As I stood watching the river, I noticed that there were some water birds [*mergos,* diving birds] tied to perches on some of the small craft [*barchis*]. Then my host went down and bound a cord about the throat of each bird; this prevented them, I learned, from swallowing the fish they caught by diving into the river.

"Next the man set three large baskets [*cistas*] in his boat, one at either end, and the third in the middle of the boat. Then he released the birds, which began to dive into the water at once. Soon they had caught many fish and filled these baskets to the top within an hour.

"Now that the baskets were full, my host released them to dive into the river without being bound around the neck. The birds fed on the fish until they had their fill. Then they finally returned to their perches as before. Later I myself ate some of the fish the birds had caught.[2]

"After a journey of several days, I chanced upon still another mode of fishing. Now the fishers were men. They had a tub filled with hot water set in the boat from which they were fishing. None of the men wore clothes (for greater ease of movement), but each had a sack tied around his neck, hanging down behind on his back. The men were diving into the water to catch the fish by hand. The swimmers kept their quarry in the sack, which they emptied into the boat as they returned to warm themselves in the tub of hot water. They took turns at this process and so caught a sizable boatload of fish."

---

2. The diving birds Odoric saw were probably cormorants; they are still used for this unusual type of fishing in some parts of China.

CHAPTER 17

The Rest of the Journey through China

 Friar Odoric pushed ever northward through the Province of Manzi. He relates his impressions of its chief city, Cansai. Except for Cambalec — and only because of the Khan's court there — Odoric's description of Cansai is the longest of any in his chronicle. Once more he used superlatives; he called it the largest city in the world, this time evidently by reason of its population more than by reason of its commerce.

The name of Cansai meant something like "royal city," rather than "heavenly city" — the definition given it by the local people. Its modern counterpart is Hangchow, which is diminished in size today, with a proportionately smaller population. As in previous cases, Odoric uses the Italian city of Venice with which to compare it. Once more Venice is smaller. The comparison of Cansai with Venice immediately suggested itself to Odoric because the

Chinese city was also built on many small islands and connected by a web of countless bridges. Odoric was told that the number of bridges exceeded twelve thousand.

The citizens of Cansai lived in what we in our time would call apartment houses. Family communes is perhaps a better term, because the system we shall describe is evidently the antique Chinese patriarchal arrangement. Three or four generations springing from one original marriage would remain together and share expenses and live under the benign authority of the pair who began the household. The patriarchal system, moreover, tended to foster the cult of ancestor worship and to engender a profound respect for age and authority, two qualities we still associate with China.

Odoric uses a technical Chinese way of expressing this communal domestic arrangement by calling it their "one fire" [*unum ignem*]. It was on the basis of the "fire," which is better translated as the "common hearth," that the annual household or property taxes were paid to the Khan. If we carry out Odoric's own multiplication of family groups or hearths, we arrive at a population of between six and nine million people in the city of Cansai and its overflowing suburbs. *"Unde multum fui miratus quot tot corpora humana poterant habitare simul"* — "wherefore I was utterly amazed that so many human beings could be packed together in one city." Yet the friar notes that there was no dearth of bread, pork, rice, and, of course, the inevitable Chinese rice wine.

As we never tire of mentioning, Odoric's interest followed a religious bent. Marco Polo's great concern was to enumerate prices, routes, salable produce, markets.

Odoric's chronicle, on the other hand, records idolatry, pagan institutions, religious and moral debasement, in order to show Europeans the natives' need for evangelization. Once more in Cansai, Odoric's main interest came to the fore in a scene which manifests the pagan belief in metempsychosis, or the transmigration of souls.

"In Cansai," Odoric dictated to the friar scribe who attended him, "four of our Friars Minor have converted a powerful man to the faith. I was visiting his home as his guest [at the time of the following incident].

" '*Atha*,' he said (which means 'Father' as a title of respect), 'would you like to see our city?'

"I replied in the affirmative. We got into a boat which took us to one of the large monasteries of the district. When we arrived, my host called out to one of the monks [on shore].

" 'You see this Frankish Raban?' my host began.[1] 'He has traveled all the way from the lands where the sun falls into the west. Now he is on his way to Cambalec to pray for the good health of the Great Khan. Why don't you show him some marvel that he can witness with his own eyes? When he returns home to his own land, he can talk about the novelty he has seen in Cansai.'

"The monk said he was glad to display some of his curiosities. He took two containers full of the leavings

---

1. Odoric was referred to as Frankish because the Franks were the most noteworthy fighters against Islam and the Tartars in the Near East and Egypt. It was also with the Franks that the Mongols had previously sought an alliance. Hence the name Frank was almost generic for all Europeans. The title of Raban meant Father, Monk, or Teacher, and perhaps all three combined. It bears a close analogy with the Biblical title of Rabbi.

of their table and led me to an enclosure, which he un-locked. The door opened into a garden (*viridarium*).

"There was a little hill covered by pleasant trees with-in this garden. As we waited, the monk took a gong [*cimbalum*] and began to sound it. With the noise of the bell, many and varied animals ran down the hillside. There were about three thousand animals all told, in-cluding apes, cats, monkeys and others, some of whose faces resembled human beings.

"The beasts arranged themselves in regular ranks around the monk, who placed the dishes of leavings be-before them and fed them as necessary. When the animals were finished eating, the monk began to sound his gong again. Then the animals returned to their hill.

"After I witnessed these goings-on, I laughed aloud with pleasure. 'What kind of animals are these?' I inquired.

" 'These animals,' replied the monk, 'are the souls of noblemen, whom we feed for the love of God.'

"I remarked that they were not souls, but simply beasts, animals.

" 'It is not true that these creatures are mere animals,' countered the monk to my remark. 'Each one of them is the soul of a nobleman. After death his soul enters into one of these beasts. The souls of peasants [*rusti-corum*], however, enter and live after death in lower forms of animal life.'

"Now I could keep on talking," Odoric concludes his story, "about many other wonders, but no one would ever believe me anyway."

Cansai was the last important stop in Manzi which Odoric describes with some detail. Then he continued ever northward and into the Province of Cathay. But the journey to Cambalec took some weeks yet. His passage through Cathay, since Cambalec lay at the northern end of it, was facilitated by his traveling most of the distance by boat, for the khans had built and maintained an artificial canal connecting the waterways of the Hoang-ho and Yangtze river systems. This Great Canal, as it was known, is one of the wonders of the Oriental world and ranks with the Great Wall of China to the north as an amazing achievement of wholesale planning and years of expense and labor.

But even these wonders could not make the friar linger. After several years of travel and previous preparation in religious life, Odoric's eyes were soon to open on the Shangri-La of his missionary dreams. Cambalec was almost in sight.

CHAPTER 18

Letters of John of Monte Corvino from Cathay

If any other name besides Odoric's deserves mention in the story of the Franciscan friars in Cathay, the name of John of Monte Corvino heads the list. Friar John left for the kingdoms of the Tartars in his early years and lived and died among them. Odoric's work was largely a missionary exploration, but Monte Corvino's work represented stability and permanence. He secured a foothold in Cambalec, and slowly unfolded the scrolls of Christian doctrine and practice to the critical eyes of the pagans and heretical Christians. His were no mass conversions. He labored for many years and added to the number of Christians little by little — yet his children can be numbered by the thousands. His steady drive and the reports of his labor, which were brought back to Europe, moved the Holy See to appoint him the first Archbishop of Cambalec. We are fortunate in having two of his letters that tell of difficulties he encountered and the slow progress he made in establishing the Church in Cathay. Friar John's two letters are classical documents in the literature of missionary endeavor.

Even aside from John's having been a foreigner and a stranger among a hostile ruling class, the difficulties he would have to meet are at once apparent. The hardest prejudices to overcome were religious. Genghis Khan, the founder of the Mongol Dynasty in China, had believed merely in some vague kind of deity, without practicing any particular recognized religious rite. It appears that several khans of Cathay and Middle Tartary were not loath to co-operating in every religious ceremony, playing safe, as it were, with all the deities recognized within their realm. Perhaps that is the reason behind the stories of the khans being baptized: we can suspect that some of them underwent baptism without any special intention of adhering to the Church's doctrine. Besides, their baptism in such a case was likely to have come from the Nestorian heretics.

The khans favored all religions as a matter of political expediency, according to the directive attributed to Genghis Khan. Perhaps this policy was also due to the usual toleration, indifference, or even contempt of spiritual values by a warrior leader who dealt in blood and power. Some of the princes favored Islam, but most of the ruling Tartars retained some vestige of their idolatrous practice, which hearkened back to the days on the steppes of the northland.

The ruling class was only superimposed on the Chinese, we must remember. The bulk of the population, before and after the Tartar conquest, belonged to groups other than the Nestorians, Mohammedans and idolaters. Some were followers of Confucius, who taught a simple belief in natural goodness. Others followed the doctrine of Lao-tse, a philosopher who taught that men were a development of primordial reason — a teaching reminiscent of ancient Greek Stoicism, but with an aggregation of superstitious rites added. The third group of religionists followed the doctrine of Buddha, which was imported from India thirteen centuries before Odoric's visit. Buddha believed in a Supreme Being and taught a very ideal system of moral enlightenment. About half a century before Odoric entered Cathay, Buddhism developed into Lamaism, a corollary of Buddhism still associated with Tibet.

These then were the established religions with which Odoric had to do battle: followers of Confucius, Lao-tse, Buddha; idolaters, Mohammedans, Nestorians, and even colonies of Jews who for centuries had preserved their racial integrity in small merchant colonies all over the Near, Middle and Far East.

Let us return in spirit to the year 1305, which was about fifteen years before Odoric arrived in Cathay. This is the year in which John of Monte Corvino wrote home to describe the foundation of his mission. The personal account given in his letters is far more interesting than half a dozen textbooks:[1]

---

1. Cf. Wadding's *Annales Minorum*, Vol. VI, pp. 77 sqq. Excerpts from both letters (the first dated January 8, the second undated) are presented consecutively here.

". . . I arrived in Cathay, the kingdom of the Tartar emperor, who is called the Great Khan. With the letters of the Lord Pope I invited him to accept the Catholic faith of our Lord Jesus Christ. But he was too accustomed to idolatry. Nevertheless, he bestowed many kindnesses on Christians. I have already been here twelve years [in 1305].

"There are Nestorians here who claim the title of Christian, even though they are far from the teachings of Christianity. They are so strong hereabouts that they prevent Christians of any other rite from setting up even a small oratory. One cannot preach any Christian doctrine save the Nestorian heresy. Yet none of the Apostles or their disciples ever came to Cathay.

"The Nestorians have persecuted me incessantly either themselves or by means of those whom they bribe with money. They say I have not been sent by the Lord Pope. I am said to be a magician, a foreign agent, and a deceiver of men. After a while they even produced false witnesses who claimed another legate had been sent [from Rome], bearing immense treasure for the emperor. But I am supposed to have killed the real legate in India and to have taken away the treasure. This lie about me persisted for about five years. As a result I was dragged to judgment several times and threatened with death [*ad judicium fui tractus cum ignominia mortis*]. At last God so disposed that some of them confessed the truth; the emperor afterward published my innocence and the wickedness of my rivals, whom he sent into exile with their wives and children.

"I was alone in this foreign land without any companion for eleven years, until Friar Arnold Alemannus of the Cologne Province arrived. He has been here for two years now. I have built a church in the city of Cambalec, which is the chief residence of the Khan. Six years ago I finished it. It has a campanile in which I have hung three bells. As I recall, I have baptized up till today about six thousand people. Were it not for the calumnies I mentioned, I would have already baptized more than thirty thousand. As it is, I perform baptisms constantly.

"I likewise have bought one hundred and fifty boys, one after the other. They are the [unwanted] sons of pagan parentage, and under seven and nine years of age. They had no training before. I have baptized them and taught them about our religion in the Latin language. I wrote out the Psalter for them, with thirty hymns and two Breviaries. Already eleven boys know the Divine Office and attend choir as it is done in our friaries [back home], whether I am present or not. Many of them are copying the Psalter and other useful texts. The emperor is very pleased with their chanting. I ring the bell for all the [canonical] hours and I pray the Divine Office with a friary full of 'infants and sucklings.' We sing the best we can, for we do not have a copy of the Office with notes.

"There was a certain king in this region, George, formerly a Nestorian, and of the family of the renowned king called Prester John.[2] The very first year I came here he took a liking to me. He was converted to the

---

2. The story of the fabulous monarch Prester John will be taken up later, at the point where Blessed Odoric himself speaks of him.

truth of the Catholic faith through me and I even gave
him minor orders. He used to serve my Mass in his
royal robes. Even though the Nestorians accused him of
apostasy, he brought a large part of his subjects to the
true faith. King George built a beautiful church with
royal generosity in honor of the Holy Trinity and of the
Lord Pope. He called it the Roman Church (to distinguish
it from the heretical Christians).

"Six years ago this King George died, a true Christian.
He left his son and heir scarcely out of his baby clothes.
Now the boy is about nine years old. The brothers of
King George, because of their own Nestorian error, led
back all whom the king converted, into their original
heresy. I was all by myself then and could not leave the
Khan's court. Therefore I could not reach that church
in the country of King George, because it is twenty days'
journey away. If only some co-operative helpers would
come, I hope in God that the Church there might be
reformed. Even now I have the right to reform it through
the permission of the late King George. . . .

"I beg my confriars who will read this letter to bring
its contents to the attention of the Lord Pope and the
Cardinals and the Procurator of our Order in the Roman
Curia. I beseech the Minister General of our Order to
send me an Antiphonal, the Lives of the Saints, the
Gradual and a Psalter with chant notation. I have only
one portable[3] Breviary and a small Missal. If I have even
one sample, the boys can copy it.

---

3. Choir books were not printed then, and one large book often
sufficed for one whole side of the choir. The pages were as large as two
feet by three feet.

"Even now I am in the process of building another church, to divide the boys into more than one group. I myself am getting old. The fact I am gray is due more to work and troubles than to old age, although I am eighty-eight years old. I am well versed in the language and script used commonly by all the Tartars. Already I have translated the whole New Testament and Psalter into the language and script of the Tartars. I had it copied in their most elegant script, from which I read and preach in open witness to the law of Christ.

"I planned with the King George I have mentioned above — had he lived — to translate the entire Office from the Latin, so that he could have it chanted all over his kingdom. Even while he was alive I celebrated Mass according to the Latin Rite in the church he built, but in the language and from the script of the Tartar people— both the words of the Canon and the words of the Preface. King George's son is, in fact, named John, after me. I hope in God that he follows in his father's footsteps. . . ."

John of Monte Corvino's second letter was written later during the same year:

"In this year of our Lord 1305, I have begun a new establishment at the very gate of the Lord Khan. There is only one street lying between us and his court — just a stone's throw from the door of his palace. Peter of Lucolongo, a faithful Christian and an important merchant from Tauris, bought the land to which I am referring and has given it to me for the love of God.

"By the providence of God, I am sure there could be no more valuable and fitting location in the whole empire of the Khan to build a Catholic church. I received the property at the beginning of last August. With the help of benefactors, by the feast of St. Francis [October 4] the wall around the property was finished, plus the cells, workshops, courtyard, and the oratory, which can hold two hundred people. On account of winter I could not complete the church. Nevertheless I have lumber piled up in the friary here, so through the mercy of God, I will finish the church this summer.

"I tell you it is a wonderful thing to see the new arrivals in the city who have not heard of our place. They see the new building and the red cross placed on top of it. They hear us solemnly chanting the Office in the oratory, even though we do not have any notes, and they are amazed. Sometimes when we sing, the Khan can hear our voices from his own room. This wonderful fact is broadcast far and wide among the people of the region, and will bear important fruit according as the goodness of God disposes and ordains."

CHAPTER 19

Cambalec

It was some time after 1322 and before 1328 that
Odoric arrived in Cambalec, to spend three years
at the Great Khan's court. His description of the
imperial court is the most lengthy in his whole
chronicle. The Oriental splendor he reveals to the
modern reader shows how far the Tartar rulers had
departed from the simple, even frugal, existence of
earlier leaders like the nomad chieftain Genghis
Khan. The splendor of the court also indicates how
the numberless Chinese have always managed to
conquer their own conquerors by absorbing them
into a higher civilization, as the Greeks did to the
Romans, softening them and rendering them unable
to cope vigorously with later incursions of other
barbarian tribes.

The Khan who was ruling when Odoric so-
journed there was a great-grandson of the legendary
Kublai Khan. His name was Yisun Timur, and he

ruled from 1323 to 1328. Even during the tenure of
Yisun Timur's celebrated great-grandfather, Kublai,
court ceremonial was elaborate and determined to the last
detail. Marco Polo records something of what he saw in
Book Two of his recollections. His story corroborates
what the friar records, and even adds sundry details not to
be found in Odoric's account, since Polo's memoirs are
longer by far.

Marco Polo, for instance, mentions the boots made of
soft white leather which visitors to the court had to wear
in the imperial household. They removed their own foot-
gear and substituted the boots provided by the Khan's
procurators, in order to keep clean and unworn the
handsome carpeting on the palace floors, which had
threads of silver and gold worked into them. Visitors
of nobility especially, Polo goes on to say, carried their
own spittoons to the Khan's residence. It was forbidden
to spit on the floor in the imperial presence. The little
vessel, therefore, was used according to its owner's needs
as long as he was actually attending the person of the
Khan. All this is reminiscent of the Oriental potentates
of whom we hear that their subjects held kerchiefs or
their mantles before their mouths in the royal presence.
This practice was observed to prevent befouling the air
which the ruler breathed.

Odoric's account is no less fascinating, and it gains,
like the other excerpts we have translated verbatim from
his chronicle, in being retold in his own words.

"The Great Khan," Odoric dictated to his scribe,
"has his capital in Cambalec. He has a huge residence
whose outer walls have a circumference of more than four

miles around. Within the wall one finds several magnificent houses of the lords of the Great Khan's family. In the midst of them all rises a hill on which is built the palace used by the Khan personally — which is the loveliest palace of the whole world. The hill itself is planted with trees. That is why they call it the Hill of Green [*Mons Viridis*].

"At one side of the hill lies an artificial lake across which runs a very charming bridge. Many wild geese, ducks and other kinds of aquatic birds live on the lake. One does not even have to leave his home here to go hunting, for the game birds are within the outer palace walls. In fact, because of several wooded enclosures on the palace grounds which are stocked with certain types of animals, one can hunt here as much as he wants, without so much as leaving the palace walls.

"The palace proper wherein the Khan resides is both immense and magnificent. It is built two paces off the ground. Twenty-four pillars of gold support the inside roof. All the walls are covered with red leather, reputed to be the finest in the world.

"In the middle of the palace there stands a huge vase, more than two paces tall. It is fashioned entirely from a precious stone called *merdatas* [evidently, jade]. It is decorated [*ligata*] around the outside with gold, and serpents [dragons] are in every corner, made to appear ferocious and threatening. Strings of large pearls, perhaps nine inches in length, hang around the vase. A liquid is channeled into this vase by pipes leading from the courtyard [*curia regis*]. They have placed containers alongside the vase for the use of whoever wishes to quench his thirst.

"One also finds many peacocks made of gold in the palace. When one of the Tartars wants to please his lord, he strikes his hands together sharply. Then the peacocks spread their wings and appear as if dancing. This is done either by the power of the devil or some kind of device underground.

"When the Lord Khan is seated upon his imperial throne, the queen is at his left. Two other wives of the Khan attend him from the step below. At the lowest step remain all the other women of the royal household. The first-born son of the king, who is destined to be the royal successor, has his place at the Khan's right hand. A little below the first-born, the other men of the royal blood attend the throne.

"Four scribes remain by the throne to record whatever the Khan happens to say. The barons and a host of other people stand before the Khan's eyes. But none of them dares to utter a single word without the Khan speaking to him first. Nevertheless, the court jesters need no such leave when they wish to entertain the Khan. Yet even they dare do nothing beyond the limits the Khan has imposed upon them.

"Barons watch at the doors of the palace to prevent anyone from touching the threshold. When someone is caught breaking this rule, he is soundly beaten (for they consider it an insult to the sanctity of the household).

"Now when the Lord Khan intends to hold a banquet, he has fourteen thousand barons serve him at table. They all wear crowns [*cum coronis*] on their heads and a garment [*vestem*], the value of whose pearl decorations is more than fifteen thousand florins! The court of the Khan is well disciplined by division into groups of ten, one hundred, and one thousand. Everyone is so assigned and answerable to his superior for his proper tasks that there is never any lack of orderliness.

"I myself, Friar Odoric, was present a good three years in the city of Cambalec. Many times was I present at such festivals, for our brethren have a place assigned to them at court. We are bound always to attend and impart our blessing. I therefore had ample opportunity to seek out and question Christians, Saracens and all the idolaters, as well as those whom we have converted to the faith, among whom there are many important barons of the court, whose duty is only to wait upon the person of the Khan. To a man, they all told me the same thing. The entertainers at court alone number some thirteen *tumans,* or about 130,000 people. Another 150,000 are engaged as kennel masters in caring for the wild animals, or as bird keepers. The health of the Khan is cared for by four hundred pagan physicians, eight Christians and one Saracen. The expenses of all these doctors are paid for from the Khan's treasury. The rest of the imperial household cannot even be numbered.[1]

---

1. Whether these barons were lords of the realm or mere palace officials is not at all certain. Their attendance upon the person of the khan may have an analogy in the functions of the nobility at one time at the courts of England and France. It is also possible that the barons, if they were actual petty nobles, were kept under the sovereign's eye at court to prevent their fomenting rebellions.

CHAPTER 20

How the Great Khan Traveled,
Hunted and Feasted

"The Khan spends summertime in a place called Sandu," continues the chronicle of Friar Odoric. "It is located at the foot of a mountain and is the most refreshing summer home in the world. In winter, of course, the Khan stays in Cambalec.

"When the Khan rides from place to place, he observes a certain procedure. He takes four armies of cavalry along. One army precedes him by a day's journey, the second and third travel a day's journey away on either side, and the fourth similarly from behind. Thus he is always moving in the center of a cross. The itinerary of each group is mapped out so that they all find the necessary provisions at each stop.

"The Khan's own retinue travels in the following manner: The Khan rides in a two-wheeled carriage, on which a beautiful chamber has been built entirely of the resinous wood of the aloes tree, ornamented with gold and set with large and costly pearls and many precious gems. Four elephants, well-matched and trained, draw the equipage, which has, besides the elephants, four noble and richly accoutered horses drawing it.

"Four barons with the title of *Zuche* travel alongside the carriage. They guard it to prevent any injury either to the carriage or to the person of the Khan. The Khan keeps twelve gerfalcons [*zirifalcos,* large and ferocious birds used for aerial hunting] near at hand in his conveyance where he sits on his throne. When he spies any birds flying past, the Khan permits the gerfalcons to attack them. Moreover, no one dares to approach the carriage within a stone's throw, except those who are charged to do so.

"Just like the Great Khan, the women of the court travel in a similar way, but each according to her own rank. Even the first-born son of the Khan observes such traveling customs. As a result, the large attendance with which the Khan moves about is unbelievable. The armies which surround him number fifty *tumans* [500,000] of soldiers. Each and every need of theirs is supplied by their lord. Should any one of the soldiers of this army die, another is appointed in his place at once to keep the number always the same....

"The Khan has his empire divided into twelve districts, each of which is called a *Syno* [or *Singo*]. One of them is the province of Manzi [described in previous chapters], which itself includes two thousand large towns. So large is the empire that if one chose to pass through all of it, exclusive of the islands of the domain, he would have to travel six months. These islands, of which there are about five thousand, are not even included in the number of the districts.

"For the sake of those who travel anywhere through his dominions, the Khan has provided hospices for their necessities. The hospices are like houses with courts called *yams*. In these houses one can find whatever is needed for human life. When something happens in the empire, at once messengers [*ambaxiatores*] rush the news on horseback to the Khan. If their business with the Khan involves difficulty and danger, the messengers use dromedaries [racing camels] instead.

"When a messenger nears the *yam,* that is, one of these houses or hospices, he blows his horn. Upon hearing the blast of the horn, the guestmaster of the hospice orders another messenger to ready himself. The first messenger gives the message he is carrying to the fresh messenger at the hospice. Then the wearied messenger can remain there to refresh himself.

"But the man who has received the message hurries on to the next *yam*. He likewise does at the next posthouse what the preceding messenger did before him. This is the way the emperor receives the news in twenty-four hours from a distance of thirty days' ordinary journey.

"The Government has another method of sending messengers on foot. Couriers are appointed to stay at houses called *chideboes*. A *chidebo* is located every three miles along the route. Each courier wears a string of bells [*nolarum seu sonaglorum*] about his waist. As he approaches the next station, the courier rings his bells loud and strong. Without any delay the next runner prepares himself to carry the message to the next station

as fast as he is able to run. All the couriers are obliged
to observe the same process until the news reaches the
Great Khan himself. As a result, nothing ever happens in
the empire without its being relayed to the Khan immediately or at least very swiftly.

"This is the manner in which the Great Khan goes to
the hunt: At a distance of twenty days' journey from
Cambalec is a verdant forest, an eight days' journey in
circumference. Enough animals of every variety inhabit
the groves to excite anyone's imagination. Wardens are
appointed to guard the boundaries of the forest in behalf
of the Great Khan.

"Every three or four years, the Khan takes his court
to the forest. When they have gathered at the forest, it
is surrounded by the attendants, who permit the dogs to
enter and who then send out the usual hunting birds.
The attendants press in closer together from all sides,
forcing the denizens of the forest to a lovely open spot
in the middle of the woods. An immense crowd of
forest animals is thus herded together — lions, deer,
buffaloes [*boves silvestres*], bears and countless other
species.

"The cries of the birds and the growling of the dogs
sent into the woods is loud enough to drown out every-
body's voice. Besides, all of the game animals are milling
about with a loud rumbling. When the beasts are all
driven to the opening in the forest, the Great Khan
approaches on the backs of three elephants. When he has
sent five arrows into the prey, the rest of the court have
their turn likewise.

"After everyone has shot his arrows — each of which is marked by its owner, in order to be distinguished from other arrows — the emperor orders the word *syo* to be called out (that is, *mercy*) to the animals which were herded together. At once the surviving animals are left to return into the woods. The courtiers then take their arrows from the slain animals. Everyone can easily recognize his own from the markings he has put on the arrows. Everyone keeps the game which has fallen under his arrows. And this is the way the Khan goes hunting.

"The emperor celebrates four great festivals each year. They are the days of circumcision,[1] his birthday, his coronation, and the anniversary of his wedding. The Khan invites all his barons, the court entertainers, and all his relatives [*omnesque de sua parentela*]. Everyone in the court occupies a place according to his rank.

"Whenever they are invited to one of these festivals, the barons wear crowns. The emperor is seated on his throne with his retinue attending him in the order described before. The barons are dressed in various colors. The first in rank are dressed in green silk; the next in

---

1. The Tartars did not practice the rite of circumcision. Perhaps Odoric was referring to the celebration of some kind of feast which fell on the date in the Tartar calendar that coincides with the Catholic feast of the Circumcision, which is also our New Year's Day. The two calendars did not show New Year's Day on the same day, so it must have been another feast. The Latin of Odoric simply reads *Festum Circumcisionis, eiusque Nativitatis diem.* Further below it reads again: *Ad festum Circumcisionis et ad festum diei Nativitatis suae.* In both cases Odoric adds a pronoun (*eius* and *suae*) only for *Nativitatis.* This seems to indicate that the feast of the Circumcision does not refer to the person of the khan, but rather to a concurring feastday of the Church.

order wear deep red [*de sanguineo*]; finally, the third group wears blue-colored clothes [*de glauco seu zamno*]. They wear crowns and a sash of gold about five inches wide [*bene uno semisse latos*], and carry a white ivory tablet in their hands. The barons stand in silence while the court entertainers wait about with their props and banners.

"In another corner of the great palace, the astrologers [*philosophi*] watch and announce certain propitious hours and moments. When the moment they have waited for arrives, one of them cries out loudly, 'Do homage to our emperor, the great lord!' Then all the barons touch their heads three times to the floor. Next the astrologer calls out, 'All of you, arise!' They all stand up at once.

"The astrologers return at other times. For instance, when the propitious moment has come, an astrologer will cry out, 'Put your finger into your ear!' — which they do. And then, 'Take it out!' — which command they once more obey. . . .

"They observe many other ceremonies which are supposed to have a deep significance. But I do not care to write of them, because they appear meaningless to us and even ridiculous.

"There are many officials of the court whose task it is to inquire whether any of the barons or entertainers has been missing. An absentee suffers a heavy penalty.

"When the propitious moment and hour for the entertainers has come, the astrologers tell the entertainers to amuse their lord. They all immediately begin to play their instruments. The singing and the uproar is enough to deafen your ears [*quod est quasi stupor unus*]. Then

someone's voice is heard: 'All of you, be silent and quiet!'
At once they are all quiet.

"The next procedure is for the relatives of the Khan
to present him with white horses. A herald cries out this
or that relative is bringing so many hundred horses for
his lord. Then these nobles reply that the horses are ready
outside the palace. The number of white horses given
the Khan in annual tribute is incredible. Next, various
barons bring gifts on behalf of others. Even the heads
of the monasteries are obliged to give the Khan their
blessing. We Friars Minor are likewise obliged to do so.

"When the presentation of gifts has been carried
out in the established order, the entertainers approach.
Some of the women sing so sweetly that it is very pleasant
to hear them. Some of the entertainers have trained
lions to make obeisance to the emperor. Finally, the
magicians cause golden cups [*ciphos*] to float through the
air. The cups are full of good wine and the magicians
can bring them to the lips of anyone who desires a drink.

"These feats and countless others are performed before the Lord Khan. To speak of them and relate the
magnificence of this lord and what happens at his court
is unbelievable for anyone whose eyes have not witnessed
them. No wonder that all this costs a great deal. Yet
the only thing paid out for money is paper bills [*cartae*],
which is used for money in Cathay. A limitless treasure
flows into the Khan's hands."

CHAPTER 21

A Long Way from Home

 Friar Odoric spent over three years at the Great Khan's court in Cathay. What he did in the way of preaching the word of God, converting and baptizing, we will know only in heaven, for that is where Odoric has willed his record to be kept. His chronicle barely hints at his own zeal and apostleship. We cannot even ascertain why he left for Italy after only three years. Perhaps his superiors had sent him merely to survey the missions in the East. Or Archbishop John of Monte Corvino may have sent him to Italy to secure more recruits.

A less adventurous soul would have returned by the more familiar water route home — the same way he had come to China. But Odoric did not know what timidity meant. He decided to travel the wilds of the Himalaya Mountains and the cold tundras of Middle Asia, back to his home. If caravans could make it through, so could he. Up to a point — as far as the immediate jurisdiction of the Great Khan extended — Odoric would be fairly safe anyway, especially if he was able to obtain a safe-conduct pass from the court officials. Otherwise, Odoric made the same preparations he had made when setting out: taking neither purse, nor scrip, nor staff, nor two tunics.

It was among a different kind of Tartar people that Odoric was going to travel now. The Mongolian Tartars of Cathay were comparatively civilized — in some respects, far superior to many Europeans Odoric knew. But outside Cambalec, the capital, the people were yet unsoftened by what historians loosely call culture: these were still the rugged, independent, nomadic tribes of the steppes of Asia. Theirs was the caliber which conquered under Genghis, proud warriors and violent politicians. Odoric would not find the same tolerant Buddhists of Cathay; the farther he penetrated toward the west, the more militant Mohammedans he would encounter, the more violent idolatry and superstition.

Out on the Gobi Desert, further north than Tibet, across the wastelands of modern Russia, the unsettled Tartars were still fighting with their lightning cavalry maneuvers that made them unconquerable. The young were yet taught to bend mighty bows strengthened with iron and horn; to ride with a heavy mace swinging from one hand and a shield bound to the opposite arm. There were no sycophants among these people, as at the court of Cathay: they still held the *divan* (their democratic council) and the *kurultai* (the gathering of the clans), to fight, to elect leaders, to mete out justice.

Odoric's previous journeys had taken him among traveling merchants and tropical peoples, absolute potentates and fabulous fortunes. What a contrast to the tents and dung fires, the bitter cold and poverty, the violence and war of Middle Tartary, which he was about to visit! On the south it was bordered by chains of mountains, on the north by the so-called Land of Darkness.

Even though the Tartars here were mostly Moslems, their orthodoxy was questionable, for they allied their primitive Tartar beliefs and practices with Islam. The Tartars did not even bother to veil and seclude their women like their western Moslem sisters. Women freely attended meals, and their association with men was more even-footed and democratic. It is not rare to hear of women who rode to war, like the Teutonic women of whom Tacitus wrote. Even if the women did not fight, their presence — and the danger to them if the battle were lost — goaded the men of the tribe to victory. Besides, on the field or in the forays, the women could nurse the wounded and cook for the army of mounted warriors.

This does not mean that the women were any the less feminine for all that. They did not sit and embroider and weave fine tapestries, like European women, Odoric saw, but they found plenty of time to stain their eyebrows, to wash in perfume, and to anoint their hair with the oil of sesame to make it black and glossy. Using oil of sesame was, in fact, a more refined beauty practice than that employed by some of the tribeswomen further west: they brought out the highlights in their hair by using camel urine for a shampoo.

Odoric lived the frugal life of the plainsmen for the several months he followed the camel caravans across Asia from Cambalec to Teheran. Perhaps his safe-conduct — if he had one — won his admittance to some of the Tartar banquets. They were rare affairs, because the tribes were always on the move after new grazing lands, but the banquets were the merrier because of their rarity, especially after a successful military campaign.

Horse meat was always on the Tartar's menu, for it was a staple food. The flesh of camels, goats, sheep and freshly caught game completed the meat courses. The Tartars had no time to coax fruits and vegetables to grow in the stubborn soil, which was arid one half the year and frozen the other half. Dairy products, especially butter and cheese, added some variety to a monotonous diet. Barley cakes and wild honey for sweetening were their main source of carbohydrates.

Except where religious practice forbade it, wine was freely drunk. But always and everywhere among Tartar peoples mare's milk was the ordinary drink. Ordinarily the milk of the mare was fermented in leather bags to make *kumys,* a potent beverage the Tartars drank as soon as they were weaned. The *kumys* was made by churning the mare's milk in leathern bags by attaching them to the riders' saddles; then the butter fat was removed to leave the rest to sour and ferment.

It is another Franciscan, who lived the century before Odoric visited Tartary, who has given historians the best description of Tartar festivals, homes and dress. This

friar's name is William Rubruk, and this is what he had
to say:[1]

> The Tartars [says Rubruk] have no permanent abodes and never
> know where they may be the next day; though every chief of a
> horde knows the bounds of his pasture grounds, and whereabouts
> he ought to be, according to the season of the year. When
> winter comes they descend towards the south, and in summer go up
> again to the cold regions of the north. The houses they inhabit
> are placed upon wheels, and constructed of a kind of latticework,
> with an opening at the top that serves for a chimney. This wooden
> frame is generally covered with white felt, plastered with lime or
> powdered bones; but sometimes these houses are black. Before
> the entrance there is suspended a piece of felt, enriched with paint-
> ings, representing flowers, trees, birds, and fantastic animals. These
> dwellings are sometimes thirty feet long, and Rubruk counted as
> many as twenty-two oxen harnessed to one of them. These great
> cabins are, however, only for chiefs; common people have much
> smaller ones, and of a conical shape, but also placed on four
> wheels; and when the tribe is on a march, the carts drawn by
> a single ox or camel are attached one to another, so that a single
> person is able to guide a long caravan of them.
>
> When the Tartars stop to encamp in any place, they always turn
> the doors of their dwellings towards the south; the master's bed
> is placed to the north, and the women occupy the eastern part; and
> a man entering the tent must take care never to hang up his bow
> and quiver on the women's side. Above the place of the head of
> the family, there is always a small image, a kind of doll made of
> felt, and called "the brother of the lord of the house," and another
> on the other side, denominated in like manner "the brother of the
> mistress." A little above, and between these two dolls, there is
> a third, a very small and meagre one, which is considered the
> guardian of the house in general. There is besides, on the women's
> side, a figure of a cow, because it is their business to milk cows;
> and on the men's, another image representing a mare, as milking
> the mares falls to the men's share.
>
> On festival days, when the Tartars assemble to drink *kumys,*
> they begin by sprinkling the image over the head of the master,

---

1. Huc, *op. cit.,* pp. 178 sqq. Huc quotes this passage from Bergeron's
Relation des Voyages en Tartarie.

and then all the others successively. A boy afterwards goes out of the tent with a cupful, and pours out a portion three times towards the south, accompanying each libation with a genuflexion. The rite is to do honour to fire; he then repeats the ceremony towards the east, the west, and the north, in honour of the air, the water, and the deceased ancestors. Before drinking, the master of the house dips his finger in the cup, and sprinkles the ground with some drops of kumys; or if he happens to be on horseback, he throws them on his horse's mane. . . .

The cotton and silk stuffs, embroidered in gold or silver, which the wealthy Tartars wear in summer, come from China and Persia; the costly furs that they wrap themselves in, in winter, chiefly from Russia and Bulgaria. Their usual plan in the winter is to wear two pelisses, one with the hair inward, the other with it turned out; and they are thus protected against wind and snow. These outer pelisses are of sheep or goat's skin for the poor, and of fox or wolf's skin for the rich; or sometimes the latter line them with silk or cotton wadding, or fine wool. The warmest kind of wool is kept for making felt, of which there is a great consumption, as it is used for carpets, for coverings for the yourtas or huts, and for cloaks to keep off the rain and snow.

The Tartar dress is in the form of a tunic, clasped always on the right side, though the Turks constantly fasten theirs on the left. The costume of the women does not differ greatly from that of the men, except that they wear a very lofty headdress, of which Rubruk enters into very minute detail, and adds: When you see a company of these women on horseback, you might take them for men-at-arms with helmet and lance, especially as they ride astride.

It is the business of the women to pitch the tents and the rolling habitations above described; to milk the cows, make the butter, prepare the skins, and sew them with thread which they make themselves from the hair of the camel or yak; and besides these employments, to make shoes, boots and garments of all kinds. They never wash their clothes, saying that God is angry if they do, and sends thunder while they are hanging up to dry. The sound of thunder terrifies them so much that when they hear it they hide themselves under their felt carpets and remain buried thus till it is over.

The men occupy themselves in making bows and arrows, saddles, bridles, bits and spurs. They take care of the camels, load and unload them for a journey, and in general look after the cattle, and tan the hides. Cleanliness is in no more favour with them than with their ladies, and their mode of washing their faces and hands is by filling their mouths with water and squirting it out over them. They never clean any of their domestic utensils, unless, indeed, when they are boiling meat; they then sometimes dip into the pot the bowls they eat from, wash them with the liquor, and then pour it back into the cauldron.

CHAPTER 22

The Roof of the World

No medieval travelogue about the East would be complete without at least a few references to Prester John. Odoric's travelogue is no exception. The territory the friar assigns to him lay west of Cathay, in the direction of Middle Tartary. Other writers, both before and after Odoric, assign his domain to Abyssinia as well as to central India. Odoric, unlike most of the other writers, refused to be fooled about the fabulous monarch, and emphatically denies the legend of Prester John's wealth and power, since he says he traveled through the land where Prester John once lived and ruled. We have already taken note of one of his descendants, King George, whom John of Monte Corvino mentioned in his letter home.

"Not a hundredth part," Odoric asserts, "of what is supposed to be indisputable fact about Prester John is actually true." Yet there was a political alliance between the Great Khan's court and Prester

John's successors, for the Khan always had one of the royal daughters of Prester John's kingdom to wife. This was no great problem because of the polygamy common to Eastern potentates.

There is a great deal to say of Prester John, but the origin of the legends about him is the initial problem that remains for historians to solve. Wishful thinking probably accounts for a great part of the legends. The people of Europe could certainly have used a Christian ally — as Prester John was thought to be — among the fierce nations of the East who were incessantly plaguing the borders of Europe. This king was said to be not only very holy and inclined favorably toward westerners, but a man of untold wealth and power, holding dominion over millions of subjects. The safest conjecture is that Prester John was one of the several Nestorian Christian potentates whom history places in the East — not very great or powerful, perhaps, but at least Christian, even though heretical. We might suspect that the reports that trickled into Europe would be magnified to present an interesting tale for troubadours and merchants to tell.

Scholars offer several possible interpretations of the origin of the name of Prester John. Some would trace the name to *Wang* in Chinese or to *Khan* in the Tartar language. We can be sure, however, that "Prester" is not a corruption of the Latin word *Pretiosus,* or "precious," as one Pope addressed him. Without doubt the name of Prester John is, by a normal rule of linguistics, a corruption of *Presbyter Joannes,* or "John the Presbyter" (meaning "priest" or "elder"). The existence of this John is based doubly: on a passage of Scripture, John 21:22f; and on some early Church writers, such as Papias and Eusebius.[1]

We can trace the beginning of the stories of Prester John to the eleventh century; the fact that Odoric has to discount the story about him in the fourteenth century indicates that legend made him even immortal. Many letters supposedly written by that royal person have been recorded in history. Whether or not several Nestorian rulers took the title of Prester John we cannot say. But we cannot doubt the existence of an original Prester, or Priest, John, even though his wealth and power were much exaggerated.

From the kingdom of the former Prester John, which was known as the territory of the Kerait Tartars, Odoric pressed southward to Tibet, which was still part of the Great Khan's domain. He called the place *Tybot,* according to the more common medieval spelling. The city which our friar made a special point of visiting is probably Lhasa, although once more we cannot be positive. But if it was, then Odoric was the first European on record to have reached the sacred and forbidden city of Lhasa in Tibet. Of course, seven centuries ago Lhasa may not have been forbidden, although the friar calls it the royal city of Tybot, well-paved [*optime scelatae*] and with walls of black-and-white construction. If the city had any lamaseries — with which the modern Lhasa is synonymous — Odoric does not name them. Yet he says the "Lo Abassi" lived here — that is, their pope, according to the Tibetan language and religious practice.

---

1. Cf. J. J. L. Ratton, *The Apocalypse of St. John,* pp. 32 sqq.

Once again Odoric leaves us a record of the pagan practices of an Eastern nation, this time the burial ceremony of Tibet, or at least its equivalent.

When a son desired to pay tribute to his father who had just died, he collected his relatives and the local priests and carried the corpse to an open field with no little merriment. The priest decapitated the corpse and presented the head to the son. Immediately everyone present began to sing and offer his prayers for the soul of the dead man.

Next the corpse was cut into small pieces and left lying alone in the field. If the birds of prey — eagles and vultures — carried off pieces of the corpse, the relatives understood it as a sign that the angels of heaven had carried the soul of the deceased into their "paradise." The son who was so honored by his father's having been taken to heaven, cooked and ate the flesh of his father's head, the skull of which was made into a drinking cup for any occasion on which to honor the dead man's memory.

The exact route taken by Odoric to the scene of his next adventure — probably the most terrifying he underwent on his whole journey by land — is a mystery. As the map indicates, however, he might have followed the valleys of the northern edge of the Himalaya. It was certainly through a valley or defile of some kind that Odoric's following adventure occurred. It is really the last personal experience that he records before his final attestation of truthfulness, and we must confess that his experience needs such an affidavit to help us believe it. We here leave the story in its original form, merely translating it, to let the reader judge for himself. At the end we offer a probable explanation.

"I had another terrifying adventure" — so runs the account dictated by the friar. "I was passing through a gorge. . . .

"In the gorge I saw an uncountable number of dead men's bones. Besides that, I heard the sound of musical instruments, especially of drums, which were mysteriously pounding. The noise was so oppressive that a horrible fear seized me.

"Now the gorge was perhaps seven or eight miles long. If any infidel entered it, he never got out alive, but perished at once. For this reason the natives of the district avoid the passage by taking a parallel route [*declinant a latere*]. But I determined to enter the valley and investigate once and for all what the cause of so many deaths might be.

"I entered the valley, as I said, and saw the remains of so many dead men that one would have had to see them to believe my story. In addition, I saw a huge and grotesque human face carved from the living rock on one wall of the gorge. I was so frightened by the appearance of the mammoth face that I honestly believe I was losing my senses because of my fear [*quod prae nimio terrore spiritum me perdere penitus credebam*].

"With a sign of the cross for protection, I repeated over and over the phrase, *the Word was made flesh*. In fact, I did not even dare to come directly up to the face carved out of the rock, but kept a distance of seven or eight paces between.

"I finally reached the opposite end of the gorge and climbed upon a sandy elevation. Although I looked carefully from all sides of the hill, I noticed nothing except for hearing the sound of the drums which continued to roll ominously. At the top of the elevation, however, I found a sizable quantity of silver coins. They were piled up as if they were no more valuable than fish scales. I took some of the silver and placed it in the folds of my habit in order to carry it away to show as a proof of my breathtaking experience. My conscience moved me to keep none of it, however, and I threw it back upon the ground. The reason why I threw all the money away on second thought is that I feared it was some kind of diabolical illusion which might have prevented my departure in safety.

"And so by the providence of God I escaped untouched. When the Mohammedans learned of my safe passage through the gorge, they respected me to the extent of calling me a specially chosen individual and even a saint [*baptizatum et sanctum*]. Whoever died in the gorge were said to be the property of the devils in hell, who play their instruments in the gorge to entice men there to kill them. I, Friar Odoric, have written of what I *saw* with absolute certainty. I have left out many other marvels because men would not believe me without seeing for themselves."

This dramatic narrative of Odoric's itinerary is not so difficult to comprehend as appears at first sight. The sound of the rolling or reverberating drums, echoing through a long and narrow defile, is a common phenomenon of nature in arid or desert regions. The shifting of sand dunes, and the attendant cracking and rumbling sounds, which are indeed most terrifying, were from time immemorial attributed to evil spirits by the natives. Note that Odoric speaks of the sandy elevation at one end of the valley; in addition, this incident evidently took place in one of the passes of the Hindu Kush Mountains, which lie at the northern edge of the Sea of Sand which Odoric encountered at Ormuz, as we mentioned in an early chapter. The noise of the shifting sands, added to the scream of the wind rushing through the narrow and rocky gorge, would have terrified any traveler. These natural phenomena may certainly have furnished the sound that passed for ominously rolling drums.

But the presence of the skeletons makes another explanation feasible. These remains point to the existence of religious ceremonies — those connected with a burial practice common in the Middle East of leaving corpses in a secluded place for carrion birds to devour; or possibly the remains indicate that robbers waylaid passing caravans or solitary travelers and left their bodies in the gorge to discourage others more superstitious than they from discovering the robber hide-out. Again, however, religious ceremonies — perhaps even human sacrifices — are indicated by the presence of the huge face carved out of the rock wall of the valley. Perhaps the pile of silver at the farther end of the gorge represented peace offerings to the supposed evil spirits, made either by travelers or by the natives who may have left their dead in the secluded valley. We shall never find out the real story, but at least we have the assurance that it was related by a Blessed of the Church, who was careful to certify what he said by a written oath — and the declaration that he would not put down the half of it for fear of being disbelieved!

CHAPTER 23

The Last Lap through Asia

Moving ever westward, Odoric now left the high tablelands north of Tibet and drew steadily nearer to the Persian Province of the Tartar Empire. Sometimes other medieval writers call the region Media, and it has caused some consternation among succeeding historians. But Media here does not have reference to the old Median Empire, but is to be understood in its literal meaning of "the middle." The territory lying halfway between China and Persia was the *terra media,* the middle land, Middle Tartary — by way of abbreviation, *Media.*

This was undoubtedly the most dangerous section of the Tartar Empire to cross. It was too far from the Great Khan to dread his influence, and too removed from any other civilized people who might have tamed the wild hearts of its inhabitants. This was the fertile spawning ground of Tartar dissension; the home of the rapacious hordes that menaced Russia and Central Europe for centuries.

Whether Odoric got through absolutely unscathed we shall never know. But at least some of his confriars shed their blood in Middle Tartary, for Islam was militant here as it had been at Tana, where the four Franciscans were martyred. Nevertheless, at least one of the friars who dared to evangelize the wild tribes of Middle Tartary — and particularly the region known as Kipchak Tartary — came out alive after being seized and maltreated. He wrote a letter from an important city of Middle Tartary, called Armalec (elsewhere, Almalic), in 1338, or scarcely ten years after Odoric passed south of the city of Armalec on his way to Persia. This daring Franciscan is known to us as Paschal of Vittoria, and we include his letter here in translation as a document of the labors and sufferings of the Friars Minor in Middle Tartary:[1]

"Friar Paschal of the Order of Friars Minor sends his greeting with every blessing to his reverend and beloved brothers in Christ, the Guardian and friars at Vittoria, and to all the dear Brethren and Fathers of the whole Custody; and not forgetful of his parents, acquaintances and friends, he sends his filial reverence.

"You all know, beloved Fathers, that I left you with our dear Father and Brother, Gonsalvus Transtorna. We set out first for Avignon. After we received the General's blessing there, we journeyed to Assisi for the [Portiuncula] indulgence.

---

1. L. Wadding, *Annales Minorum*, Vol. VII, pp. 256 sq.

"We embarked at Venice in a freight ship [*carraca*] and sailed down the Adriatic Sea and toward the Sea of Pontus. We sailed along Greece — that is, Galatia, with Sclavonia at our left and Turkey at our right. At Constantinople we met our Father, who is the Vicar of Cathay in the vicariate of the East.

"We crossed the Black Sea in a little craft. The bottom of this sea is so deep that it cannot be sounded. So we reached Gazaria in the Northern Vicariate of the Tartar Empire. Then we passed over another bottomless sea to reach Thana.

"Because I arrived ahead of my companions, I set out for Sarai with some Greeks in their wagons. Actually, my brothers got as far as Urganth. I wanted to go after them, but after some consideration I determined to learn the language of the country. By the grace of God I did learn the speech of the Cumani and how to write in Vigurian. These two languages are commonly used throughout the Tartar Empire, in Persia, Chaldea, Media and Cathay.

"My companions came back from Urganth, determined to return home. But I refused to return, as it were, like a dog to its vomit [*ad vomitum abhorrens redire*]. Besides, I desired the blessing of the Holy Father. All of us friars who have come to these foreign lands have the same indulgence as if we had pilgrimaged to Jerusalem, that is, *plenissima a poena et culpa.* And to those who persevere in grace till the end of their lives, the crown of life will be given.

"It is for this reason, Fathers, and because I knew the language, that by the grace of God I have often preached

the word of God without an interpreter to the Mohammedans, as well as to the Christians, schismatics and
heretics. Besides, I have the order from my Vicar, whom
I have mentioned above, to the mission I had begun, in
virtue of my vow of obedience, to be accomplished as
soon as I had read his letter.

"Now I had spent more than a year in the city of
Sarai, a Mohammedan town belonging to the Tartar
Empire in the Northern Vicariate. Three years earlier one
of our friars, named Stephen, suffered a holy martyrdom
at the hands of the Mohammedans there.

"Embarking on a small boat with some Armenians,
I traveled on the Volga River and along the shore of the
Caspian Sea till I reached Sarachuk. Then I used a
carriage drawn by camels to continue my journey, because
to *ride* a camel is a fearful thing indeed. On the fiftieth
day I reached Urganth, which is on the border between
the [Middle] Tartar and Persian empires. The place is
also called Hus; and it is where the body of the holy Job
lies buried.

"Once again I got into a camel-drawn carriage, this
time with some accursed Agareni, followers of Mohammed. I was the only Christian among them. With my
attendant Zinguus, I reached the empire of the Medes
[the Middle Empire of Tartary] under God's guidance.
What kind and how many torments I suffered here, God
alone knows. It would take too long to describe in a
letter. The emperor of Middle Tartary was slain by his
brother, and the caravan with which I was traveling was
held up in the towns of the Mohammedans, for fear of
war and of being plundered.

"That is how it happened that I was delayed a long time among the followers of Islam. I preached the name and gospel of Jesus Christ many days in succession, openly and in the sight of all. I exposed the deception of their false prophet, his fraud and blindness. I shamed their wrongdoing [*latratus*] loudly and publicly. Trusting in the Lord, Jesus Christ, I feared them very little, because the Holy Ghost strengthened and enlightened me.

"They set me before their mosque during their 'Easter' celebration. Because of the festival many *Cadini,* that is, their bishops, and *Talismani,* their priests, were gathered from distant regions. I disputed with them under the guidance of the Holy Ghost for twenty-five days in that very place — before the doors of their mosque — about holy topics and about their false doctrine and their Koran. I scarcely had time even to eat bread and water once each day.

"By the grace of God I preached and revealed the doctrine of the Holy Trinity, which even they had to admit unwillingly at the end. Thanks to God, I was successful in all the disputes, to the praise and honor of Jesus Christ and Holy Mother Church. But these sons of the devil tempted me with gifts. They promised me women, virgins, gold and silver, goods, horses and cattle, and all the other pleasures of the world to turn my mind.

"When I spurned their advances, for two days I suffered stoning; they put fire to my face and my feet. They pulled out the hairs of my beard; they inflicted blows, names and ignominy on me for a long time. God, Who is all-blessed, and through Whom I observe the life of poverty, knows that I rejoiced and was glad in the Lord,

Jesus Christ. He knows in His wonderful holiness that I deserved to suffer for His name.

"Behold how God has led me to the city of Armalec in the Middle Empire, in the vicariate of Cathay, beginning from Urganth, the last city between Persia and Tartary. Along the way I spent five months alone among the Mohammedans, carrying about the name of Jesus Christ by word and example and the habit I wear. Often they gave me poison to drink. They threw me into water. I bore their blows and other torments which my letter cannot mention.

"Still I thank God in all things. I am now waiting to suffer yet worse things for His name and for the remission of my sins, that I may safely reach the kingdom of heaven by loyalty to God. Amen.

"Farewell in Jesus Christ and pray for me and for all those who are making or intend to make this missionary journey. By the intervention of God, this mission is of great value in reaching and harvesting many souls. Do not look to see me any more, except if you come to these foreign lands, or in paradise, where there is rest, consolation and His presence, our inheritance, our Lord, Jesus Christ. He Himself has said, wherever this gospel is preached throughout the whole world, it is the fulfillment of the world's purpose [*consummatio saeculi*].

"Therefore, dear brethren, it is mine to preach among the various nations, to bring forgiveness to sinners, to point out the way of salvation. But it is God's to pour down the grace of conversion.

"Given at Armalec, in the Middle Empire, on the feast of St. Lawrence, in the year of our Lord 1338."

Such was the caliber of the men to whose religious fraternity Friar Odoric belonged. The letter of Friar Paschal of Vittoria barely hints at what the friars had to endure at the hands of the infidels.

The first city of Persia to which Odoric's itinerary took him was the familiar Soltania, mentioned in the account of Odoric's journey out to Cathay as the seat of the Khan of Persia's summer palace. It was at this point that Odoric found himself following the same route that he took out on the journey from the Black Sea — only this time his face was turned away from Cathay. It would be just a short voyage to Italy and home.

But before Odoric closes his chronicle, he has to give a backward sweeping glance to the work of his confriars in Tartary. What shall he say of them in commendation?

What struck him most of all as an attestation of the holiness of their work and, more fundamentally, the need of their work, was the exorcisms performed by the Franciscans in Tartary. The exorcisms were the symbols of the victory over the powers of darkness by these crusaders of light. Odoric boldly asserts that those who asked for baptism after being exorcised were many. In fact, he says that casting out devils was as common and ordinary there as putting the dog out of the house anywhere else.

Like Boniface in Germany, the friars scorned the national deities. These were little dolls of felt, and the friars cast them into a fire. Sometimes, at the instigation of the devil, the felt dolls leaped from the flames. But a liberal dose of holy water on the fire itself chased the evil spirits from their fiery element. When the friars threw them back again, the images of felt burned, to the dismay — and often to the conversion — of the Tartar men and women.

At times the Evil One voiced his anger and pain, crying out aloud to the bystanders: "Look! Look how I am cast out of my own house!" This was the open confirmation that the worship of idols — especially as the principle of evil — is the worship of the devil himself. Liberals and rationalists may laugh, but they have not locked horns with the archenemy of God.

And so ends the chronicle of Friar Odoric, the Bohemian — but not yet his life story.

CHAPTER 24

Home at Last

Fourteen years is a long time in anyone's life. For Odoric, the last fourteen years of his life represented his life in religion, his life spent as missionary, his life of exile. His return offered him no solace, because it was a return to a Christendom divided by irreligious politicians and politically-minded religious. The Pope was still at Avignon, more than ever the tool of the French monarch. The division had its counterpart within the Order of St. Francis itself.

From 1328 to 1330 — the year of Odoric's return — Nicholas V, the Franciscan antipope appointed by Louis the Bavarian, reigned in opposition to John XXII. He created many prelates and divided the faithful in their allegiance, instead of solving the problem of Peter's successor, as he had hoped to do. Later he submitted in good faith to the Pope's mercy and died in honorable confinement.

At the same time (from 1329 to 1330) the wicked and notorious Michael Cesena, a deposed General of the Order, leagued himself with the Ghibellines against papal authority, causing no end of political agitation. It was all the worse for being masked under the guise of religion.

The third cause of division within the Order that Odoric faced upon his return were the so-called Spirituals. Angelo da Clareno was their leader. The Spirituals obtained leave from Pope Celestine V to live apart from the conventual friaries. They were something of ascetics and something of heretics. But in the long run, there was little difference between their uncompromising attitude and the stubbornness of the early Christian Encratites and Montanists.

After alternate favor and disfavor by the Church and by the Order, Angelo da Clareno, in the very year of Odoric's return, published a defense of his actions in the *Historia Septem Tribulationum*. This apologetic work tells of the seven stages of suffering to be borne by the only true followers of Francis, among which he numbers his own persecution by the Order. Angelo's adherents were many and powerful. Accusations and decretals were thrown back and forth from either side. Only about twenty years later were the Spirituals and their more pernicious allies, the Fraticelli, stamped out of the Order and out of the Church.

An antipope, notorious anti-papal politicians, heretical sects — these unworthy Franciscans were tearing the seamless garment of Christ and the Order to shreds at the very moment Odoric disembarked at Venice. No pleasant greeting was this, but still no reason to quit the field of battle. But we may rightly doubt whether all of Odoric's petitions for his beloved mission field evoked much enthusiasm in the Pope or the General of the Order. The barques of Christ and Francis were on the rocks and unmanned at home. The agitation of religious rigorists and ambitious politicians, using the Church for temporal ends, had reached a climax during the friar's absence of fourteen years. Armies were marching down from Germany and up from Sicily.

And yet it remained true that the pagodas of Cathay, the temples of Mobar, and the tents of Tartary needed opening to the true God, and Blessed Odoric would not be denied. His constant resolve was to turn his face to Cathay once more, followed by a troop of valiant friars whose sandaled feet were anxious to blister in the desert and freeze on the northern plains.

Such was the plan and intention of Odoric; Providence had another idea from all eternity.

Odoric returned and immediately visited his native march of Treviso and Friuli. His face was so changed by the squalor and famine he had suffered, so darkened by exposure to the elements, that his own parents refused to believe he was their son.

His next step was to visit Pope John XXII at Avignon for permission to return to Cathay with fifty friars from any of the provinces. But illness and frailty, after a fourteen years' chase, finally caught up with him at Pisa. One manuscript reads that it was here an old man appeared to Odoric, greeted him and walked at his side.

"Who are you?" the friar asked politely.

The answer came, as if in reproach for Odoric's ignorance. "Why, I knew *you* even when you were traveling far away from home in India. Yes, I watched you and your holy way of life."[1]

Having advised Odoric of his approaching death, and instructed him to return to Udine, the old man disappeared. Although Odoric did not feel ill at the time, he complied at once. When he was back in the Paduan Province, the first indications of his final illness forced him to bed. Then it was that his Provincial Minister, Guidotto, ordered him to dictate the chronicle of his missionary journey, from which we have drawn so much of this biography.

Odoric made a general confession on his deathbed. It is told of him that he received an assurance of his salvation, yet he told his confessor:

"Use the [sacramental] power that has been conferred on you, reverend Father. Even though the Lord has given me a sign that He has already forgiven me all my sins, yet I wish to submit myself as a humble client to the keys of the Church."

---

1. Another manuscript makes out the old man to be St. Francis, whose words were supposed to have been: "I will go [to Avignon] for you and your business and take care of what your heart desires. But do you take courage and rise; return to your little nest [Udine]. You will die there, and not in this city [Pisa], which has set itself against the Pope to such a degree that it is not worthy to hold you even when you are dead." This last part strongly suggests having been written by someone of the papal party — probably one of the friars — who was criticizing Pisa, which was a Ghibelline city.

A little while after he received the Last Sacraments, Blessed Odoric placidly fell asleep in the Lord. Just forty-six years old, he was through with traveling; he had found his Home at last.

It was a Monday, about three o'clock in the afternoon, on the fourteenth day of January, 1331.[2]

2. For the account of his death, the miracles performed by his intercession, and the great confluence of pilgrims to his shrine, as well as for an outline of his itinerary, see Wadding's *Annales Minorum*, Vol. VII, pp. 144-148.

APPENDICES

BIBLIOGRAPHY

INDEX

APPENDICES

I

DECLARATION OF HENRY OF GLATZ

Attesting to the reliability of the chronicle

(From the *Acta Sanctorum*)[1]

"AND I, FRIAR HENRY OF GLATZ, HAVE TRANSCRIBED ALL of the foregoing narrative while I was at Avignon in the court of the Lord Pope during the above-mentioned year [1331]. If I had not known there the blessed Friar Odoric and the companions who were with him, as well as the perfection and labor of his holiness, I could hardly have believed any of the things described herein. But the truthfulness of his life forces me to give credence to his words. I have written this in the year of our Lord 1340 in Prague, near the feast of All Saints. And more than all this did I hear when I was in Avignon."

---

1. See Yule-Cordier, *op. cit.,* Vol. III, p. 277.

II

EULOGY OF BLESSED
THOMAS OF TOLENTINO

(From the *Breviarium Romano-Seraphicum,* in the Office of
Blessed Thomas)

THOMAS of Tolentino was born in Piceno of noble parentage. Inflamed with the desire to become perfect, he entered the Franciscan Order in his early adolescence. He was outstanding for his love of poverty and zeal for the salvation of souls.

His superiors destined him for the mission fields of the East. First in Armenia, then in Persia he led countless schismatics back to union with the Church, and convinced a great number of pagans to profess the teachings of Christ.

Thomas also acted as a papal legate, and earned the approval of Pope Clement V. On the strength of his testimony the Pope made John of Monte Corvino, a zealous missionary, the first Archbishop of Cambalec (Peiping) and the representative of the Holy See in the whole of the empire of China. Besides, the Pope gave John of Monte Corvino seven suffragan bishops who constituted the hierarchy there.

Thomas returned a third time to the Orient, with the idea of a new expedition among the Tartars and Indians. He set out for Cola, but unfavorable winds brought him to Tana. He died there by decapitation, as glorious martyr, on April 9, 1321.

His holy body was carried by Blessed Odoric to the church of the Friars Minor in Zayton. The relics of the martyr's head were brought to Tolentino, where they are piously venerated. Pope Leo XIII ratified and confirmed the cult paid to Blessed Thomas from time immemorial.

III

POPES WHO REIGNED DURING BLESSED ODORIC'S LIFETIME
(1285-1331)

1. Honorius IV, 1285-1287
2. Nicholas IV, 1288-1292 (Franciscan Pope)
3. Celestine V, July (Aug.) 1294-Dec. 1294
4. Boniface VIII, 1294-1303
5. Benedict XI, 1303-1304
6. Clement V, 1305-1314
7. John XXII, 1316-1334
8. Nicholas V, 1328-1330 (antipope)

IV

CARDINAL PROTECTORS

1. Matthew Rossi, 1279-1306
2. John Mincio of Murrovalle, 1306-1312
3. Arnold of Pelagrua, 1313-1334

V

MINISTERS GENERAL
OF THE ORDER OF FRIARS MINOR

1. Arlottus of Prato, 1285-1286
2. Matthew of Aquasparta, 1287-1289
3. Raymond Gaufredi, 1289-1295
4. John Mincio of Murrovalle, 1296-1304
5. Gonsalvus of Valboa, 1304-1313
6. Alexander Bonini, 1313-1314
7. Michael Fuschi, 1316-1328
8. Gerald Eudes, 1329-1342

VI

IMPERIAL HOUSES OF CHINA
DURING THE MIDDLE AGES

T'ang Dynasty: 618-907
The Five Small Dynasties: 907-960
Sung Dynasty: 960-1279
Yüan (Mongol) Dynasty: 1279-1368
Ming Dynasty: 1368-1644

(See Chronological Tables in *Documented History of the Franciscan Order,* by Raphael Huber, O. F. M. Conv.)

BIBLIOGRAPHY

Brinkley, F., *China, Its History, Arts and Literature,* Vol. X. Boston: J. B. Millet Company, 1902.

De Gubernatis, D. a Sospitello, *Orbis Seraphicus, Pars Secunda.* Rome, 1689.

Elogio storico alle gesta del Beato Odorico dell'Ordine de' Minori Conventuali con la storia de lui dettata de'suoi viaggi Asiatici. Venice: Antonio Zatta, 1761.

Eubel, C., *Provinciale O. F. M. Vetustissimum.* Quaracchi, 1892.

Huber, R., *Documented History of the Franciscan Order.* Milwaukee: The Nowiny Publishing Apostolate, Inc., 1943.

Huc, l'Abbé (Evariste Régis), *Christianity in China, Tartary and Thibet,* Vol. I. New York: D. and J. Sadlier and Company, 1887.

Komroff, M., reviser and editor, *The Travels of Marco Polo,* Marsden's translation. New York: Modern Library, 1931.

Lamb, H., *Genghis Khan.* New York: Garden City Publishing Company, 1927.
— *Tamerlane.* New York: Garden City Publishing Company, 1928.

La Monte, J., *The World of the Middle Ages.* New York: Appleton-Century-Crofts, Inc., 1949.

Maas, O., *Franciscans in the Middle Kingdom.* Tientsin, 1938.

Mann, H. K., *The Lives of the Popes in the Middle Ages,* Vol. XVII. London: Kegan Paul, Trench, Trubner and Company, Ltd., 1931.

Ratton, J. J. L., *The Apocalypse of St. John*. London: R. and T. Washbourne, Ltd., 1912.

Thauren, J., *Atlas der katolischen Missionsgeschichte*. Moedling (bei Wien): Missionsdruckerei Sankt Gabriel, 1932.

Wadding, L., *Annales Minorum,* Vols. V-VII. Quaracchi, 1931-1932.

Yule, H., *Cathay and the Way Thither,* Vols. I-IV, new ed. by H. Cordier. London: Hakluyt Society, 1913-1916.

INDEX